121 *INTERNET* BUSINESSES YOU CAN START FROM *HOME*

PLUS

A BEGINNER'S GUIDE TO STARTING A BUSINESS ONLINE

121 *INTERNET* BUSINESSES YOU CAN START FROM *HOME*

PLUS

A BEGINNER'S GUIDE TO STARTING A BUSINESS ONLINE

Ron E. Gielgun

Actium Publishing, Brooklyn, New York

Printed in the United Stated of America by Bookmart Press, Inc

2 3 4 5 6 7 8 9 10   98 99

Publisher's Cataloging-in-Publication
(*provided by Quality Books, Inc.*)
Gielgun, Ron E.
        121 Internet businesses you can start from home : plus a beginner's guide to starting a business online / Ron E. Gielgun.
        p. cm.
        Includes index.
        ISBN 0-9657617-3-8

        1. Internet (Computer network) 2. Business enterprises--Communication systems.
        3. New business enterprises--Data processing. 4. Home-based businesses. I. Title
        II. Title: One hundred twenty-one Internet businesses you can start from home.
        III. Title: One hundred and twenty-one Internet businesses you can start from home.

HD30.37.G54 1997   025.06'65
                        QBI97-40454

                Library of Congress Catalog Card Number: 97-72020

Table of Contents:

Preface

The Internet is growing at an astounding rate. Billions of dollars are already changing hands online. More and more people are doing at least some of their shopping on the Internet, and an increasing number of conventional businesses are establishing a presence online in order to tap into this new market. The business community is only now beginning to explore the limitless opportunities that the Internet offers them. Starting a business on the Internet is easy, affordable, and does not require you to learn computer programming.

This book was written for people who want to start their own business on the Internet. Without resorting to complex technical terms, it deals with all aspects of operating an online business — from establishing a virtual storefront to marketing your products/services online.

It is a good idea to log on to the Internet (through a basic dial-up account) before you start planning your Internet business. It will be a lot easier to plan an Internet business site after you have explored the Internet, visited hundreds of sites, and taken advantage of the vast pools of information the online world offers.

Ron E. Gielgun

Disclaimer

This book is sold with the understanding that the publisher and author are not engaged in rendering legal, accounting or other professional services. It is designed to provide information about the subject matter covered. It is not the purpose of this book to reprint all the information that is otherwise available to the author and/or publisher. The text in this book should be used only as a general guide and not as the ultimate source of information for the subject matters it covers.

At no event shall the author or Actium Publishing be liable or responsible for any loss or damage caused, or alleged to be caused, to any person or entity, directly or indirectly by the information contained in this book. In spite of the effort that has been made to ensure the accuracy, quality, currentness, validity and suitability of the information written in this book, there may be mistakes, both typographical and in content. The information in this book is not warranted or guaranteed in any way.

Product or brand names used in this book may be trade names or trade marks. These names have been used in an editorial manner without any intent to convey endorsement of or other affiliation with the name claimant. The author and the publisher express no judgment as to the validity or legal status of any such proprietary claims.

SECTION I

STARTING A BUSINESS ONLINE

CHAPTER 1

DOING BUSINESS ON THE INTERNET

The Internet and the Media Hype

"Get your business on the Internet *now* or you'll miss out on the gold rush of the twentieth century," the media seems to continuously tell us whenever we turn on a TV or open a newspaper. We hear this message from talk show hosts and guests, news reporters, even serious economists and business people. It seems that the rest of the business world — those unfortunates who do not have a Web site — are doomed to oblivion, about to make room for what, we are promised, is soon to be the only game in town.

To what extent is this widespread prediction true? The business of the news media, let us remember, is to make news. Hype and journalistic enthusiasm can sometimes replace professionalism, so long as it proves to increase rating or circulation. Let us see things as they are: conventional businesses do not face extinction should they decide to ignore the online world. Local businesses will continue to thrive even without an online presence. Most of them would benefit little or not at all from having an Internet site. The time is yet to come when orders for pizzas, taxis, and plumbers are processed *mainly* through the Internet. For all we know, such an age may never arrive at all.

However, to give the online world its due, there is a grain of truth in the media hyperbole. The Internet is *in* and even by the very fact of attracting the millions of consumers and businesses that it has, it has created a huge new market for entrepreneurs to exploit. Money does change hands in the online world, and an increasing number of people are making a living out of it. One of the Internet's best features is its unbelievable growth rate. Currently, over 40,000,000 people are reported to be connected to the net, and this figure is up from about 8,000,000 in 1993 and from only several thousands in the early nineteen eighties. 100,000,000 people are projected to be connected to the Internet by the end of the decade, and the number is likely to keep growing, creating what is probably to become the largest market in history. Indeed, many consumers are going to pour money into the Internet; but just how much money?

It seems that wherever we go people talk of Internet millionaires and sixteen-year-old computer geeks who have become filthy rich overnight without ever bothering to get up from their computer desks. Every business around us seems to have already found its way to the Internet — even cemeteries. But are they all going to make millions on the net?

Well, no. Naturally, as in any other business, some skillful entrepreneurs who came at the right time with the right idea have, and will, make fortunes. However, the online world is just a reflection of the real world. Internet subscribers do not constitute a new consumer group which had hitherto never existed. Most of them, although on average more affluent than the rest of the population, do not have unlimited amounts of money to spend on online shops, and many are young students. Just as in real life, some of the businesses on the Internet will make a lot of money, most will make *some* money, and a certain number will eventually go out of business.

Only by understanding this — that a business on the Internet is not that much different from conventional businesses, that it is subjected to almost the same market laws and trends — can we hope to succeed, and make a living on the Internet. It is possible; it is as easy to make a living out of the Internet as it is to make a living out of most conventional businesses. The rules are almost the same: your degree of success depends on your investment in time and (wisely) money, business ideas, professionalism, perseverance, and luck. One outstanding difference between the conventional and online business worlds, however, does exist: the rule "*Location, Location, Location*" does not apply to the Internet; its place is taken by "*Promotion, Promotion, Promotion.*"

The Internet is not a get-rich-quick-scheme, but there are many advantages to starting a business there:

➤ Start-up capital can be relatively low. Most Internet businesses (and the business ideas in Section II) can be operated from your own home, and you will not need to rent commercial space. In addition, the overhead tends to be lower for most online businesses.

➤ Flexible location. Most Internet businesses will allow you to live wherever you want, since almost any Internet site can be reached from anywhere in the world.

➤ Huge international potential. The Internet allows you to reach people from all over the world: foreign corporations, potential tourists, investors, consumers — and all at the same cost of reaching your next door neighbor. This is an important advantage in a world that moves towards economic globalization.

➤ An incredible growth rate, equaled by no other market. Even if you are competing for a particularly small niche in the market, the number of potential costumers for your business will probably double or triple in a very short time. One of the reasons so many businesses are now in a frenzied hurry to set up shop on the Internet, even if they know they can at best hope to break even, is that being among the first counts. Suppose, for instance, that you hope to sell boat accessories online. The market for these accessories is currently small, and you can hope to sell only a few. In a few years, as the market for these items grows, more businesses like yours will no doubt open up shop on the Internet. However, by then most every potential customer with either an online access or a friend with an online access will probably have heard of you, and will keep you in mind whenever she needs boat accessories. This will give you a definite edge over your competitors in the (by then) already large online boat accessories market.

➤ Convenient hours. You don't have to maintain regular business hours. Most Internet sites work without human intervention, and the required business activity (i.e. processing payments, maintaining the site) can be done at your own time. For many

Internet businesses, you will not even be required to quit your day job.

➤   New venues for promotion. Promotion on the Internet, although not to be relied upon solely, will connect you to costumers who would never have found you otherwise. The best thing about it — most of the online promotion options are absolutely free.

➤   The ability to run two or more businesses simultaneously. Some Internet businesses require so little time and investment that you can easily operate two or more such businesses, thereby increasing your income in a way which would never have been possible with any conventional business.

➤   Distributing information electronically costs a lot less than hard copy (paper) distribution. Catalogs and information packages about your products can be distributed to prospects at no recurring printing cost to you and no mail or fax charges.

➤   Flexibility in changing to another type of business (should the need arise). If one type of business proves unprofitable for any reason, you can easily switch to another, and without the hassle of breaking leases and changing locations.

➤   Starting an online business is easier than starting most conventional businesses. Many (but not all!) of the preparations involved can be done without leaving your desk.

➤   The Internet mentality is content based. What Internet customers require is accurate, concise information about your products. In other words, you don't have to put on a phony smile for every prospect who enters your online site. You still have to work hard to ensure the success of your business, but you don't have to be a born salesman.

➤   The government has made a commitment to the Information Super Highway, and has already invested billions of dollars in developing communication networks. Opening a business on the Internet now will be the equivalent of opening a gas station near one of the (then new) highways the government paved during the fifties. It would be like sowing a field that someone else has already plowed.

So, while having a business presence on the Internet does not by itself guaranty that the entrepreneur will strike it rich, it is definitely an enterprise worth trying. It may change your life for the better, and give you more flexibility in time management and choice of a place to live. If you have the right idea or product, if you learn how to exploit the advantages the Internet can give your business, there is no reason why you should not make a lot of money online. However, keep in mind that operating a business on the Internet requires the same dedication, perseverance, and struggle for success that any conventional business would. Many Internet entrepreneurs have allowed themselves the erroneous assumption that, if well designed and paid for, an Internet site *must* work for them without any further intervention, and without gumption and initiative on their part. You cannot expect your online business to make you money just by being connected to the Internet. Problems and difficulties are bound to arise, as they do with any business, and you will have to make a commitment in time, money, and work.

Some of the online entrepreneurs who failed did so because they invested too much money in a market that was still too small to allow for an adequate return on their large investments. Remarkably, some of these latter entrepreneurs were huge corporations, (CBS, for one) who invested millions of dollars in online projects and found themselves either dropping out of online ventures altogether, or at best not making any money on them. As a small entrepreneur, your main asset is your flexibility — the ability to react fast and adapt quickly to new Internet trends and whims. You can do what huge corporations can never do — operate a business at minimum expenses, and reach decisions quickly.

The Online Consumer

Who is the online customer? Internet demographics tend to be inaccurate and surveys vary in their conclusions. It is hard even to say with any degree of certainty how many people actually have access to the Internet. We may know the number of subscribers (and even such data is not certain, as there is no Internet headquarters to organize and centralize such information), but the number of subscribers correspond to the number of computers that are connected to the Internet and not to the number of people that use these computers. The actual number of people who use the Internet is therefore an educated guess at best. A cross section of the Internet population is even harder to assemble, and different surveys yield different statistics.

What we *can* gather from these statistics are these facts:

1. Between 60 and 80 percent of Internet users are males.

2. The vast majority of Internet users fall between the ages of 18 and 45.

3. This is an affluent group; between 80 and 90 percent of Internet users earn at least $25,000 a year.

4. Most have a college degree.

5. About half are married.

6. About two thirds live in the U.S.

7. More than half are connected through commercial servers. The rest are divided between academic, research, government and military networks. The proportion of commercial connections (which reflects private users) is growing steadily.

Keep in mind, however, that these figures are based on computer owners' demographics as well as Internet users'. It is assumed that all Internet subscribers own or have access to a computer, although a few manufacturers recently came out with online terminals that are not PCs.

Most surveys refer only to private users, but many Internet users are students, who use their school/universities' connections. They spend a long time browsing the net and its sites, but rarely have the money to pay for the products and services they come across there. They should not be dismissed as non-consumers, however — an increasing number of online businesses make their living from advertising charges. As we will discuss later, attracting and recording as many "hits" (Internet users who have entered your site/pages) as possible is a goal unto itself.

The Online World: Mentality

From time to time, new infrastructures and foundations are being laid to allow for the future development of society. Investors, whether government or private, lay those foundations with one of these two goals in mind:

1. To allow for future expansion of businesses/industry and to aid the overall growth of the economy. Some of these foundations were created by the private sector, but most are laid by governments. Examples are railway systems, communication satellites, ports and airports, dams and power plants. All these ventures are commercially oriented.

2. To help certain government entities to fulfill their functions — mostly defense, social or educational. Investment in these kinds of foundations also carries with it a tremendous economic boost. Examples: the jobs created by military industries; the utilization of government-sponsored research by private industries; and of course the skilled work force turned out by the educational system. The foundations and investments in this category, although often extremely beneficial for the growth of the economy, were not created by the private sector and are all controlled by non-profit organizations. They do not have to be in the black and often do not have to show any immediate results. Their mentality is non-commercial. <u>The Internet belongs in this category</u>.

The Internet, as the next chapter will explain, was created in the height of the cold war for strictly defensive purposes. Universities and research institutes joined it later for the opportunity of quick exchange of information it provided them. The commercial onslaught on the Internet began only during the mid 1980s, when the growing popularity of the PC finally enabled many individuals to log on to the Internet.

The Internet mentality has so far managed to remain non-commercial. That is not to say that businesses would never prosper online, but it does mean that the attitude towards potential customers should be completely different from that of the conventional business world. The Internet is still an open field, a virgin soil for entrepreneurs that is yet unbound by excessive regulation and central control. The mentality, or culture, of the online world populace has developed accordingly.

We can draw a few lines to the Internet consumers' mentality:

1. They are more community-oriented than conventional consumers. If Internet users feel that they have been "gypped" or are otherwise unsatisfied with an online business, they can immediately use the newsgroups and e-mail services at their disposal to spread the word to any potential online customers. The same is true for conventional businesses — the Internet has turned out a new generation of educated consumers who would not hesitate to warn the online community of any business, online and conventional, they had had a bad experience with. There are even newsgroups that have been started solely for the purpose of dealing with one product or one company, and potential buyers are learning to browse these newsgroups' postings when they contemplate the purchase of the product.

    It is also much harder to give disinformation to the online consumers, since they have immediate access to the Internet's vast information resources. In a nut shell — it is much easier for online consumers to reach one another than it is for conventional consumers.

2. What the Internet subscribers crave most of all is information. Advertising on the net should be treated in the same manner — it has to be content-based. Hyperbole and glitzy car-dealers' selling approach would not move the goods here. Online consumers demand the facts, not subliminal messages and image-based promotions.

3. The Internet is interactive and users would like it to stay that way. TV or magazine style advertisements would never work here. Visitors to an Internet site or a virtual storefront must be

given the opportunity to contact you, the online business, with any questions and criticism they might have, and you had better be ready to give them a quick reply.

4. Internet consumers want to have everything *now*. If, for example, your virtual storefront displays three kinds of electronic scales for sale, your potential customers would probably want to see all available information on all of them at the click of the button. There is no point in setting up an Internet presence if your customers are to be sent conventional brochures through the mail. If they decide to order one of your scales, they would also want to do it right away — within a minute if possible. If you tell your customers that your electronic scales have received excellent reviews in a certain online magazine — allow them to link to these magazines' sites immediately. Your site must enable your potential customer to do everything at the click of a button.

5. Internet users are obsessed with the new. Unlike other media ads, which may remain unchanged for months, Internet business sites must be constantly changing and renewing.

6. The Internet world is international. Your next door neighbor can of course reach your site, but so can a resident of Japan — and with the same ease. If you believe that your products or services have an international appeal, don't forget to dedicate a section of your site to dealing with foreign visitors' special needs (such as shipping or language).

7. The online community guards its privacy and valuable time fervently. Conventional telemarketing techniques do not go over well; they may also prove to be counter productive. Unsolicited mass e-mailing can only lead to angry protestation from your potential costumers, who may e-mail bomb you in retaliation — a process known as flaming. You will probably lose more customers using such methods than you gain.

8. The anonymity and reach-the-whole-world-at-the-click-of-a-button attitude with which the Internet endows its users causes some of them to abandon all sense of proportion and conduct,

and fills them with illusions of grandeur and self confidence. When these immature users (mostly juvenile) have a complaint about some of your products or services they will send you hate e-mail. Foul language and death treats are not uncommon responses even when the problem they are out to denounce is no more than a print error, missing graphics or a wrong link on your site. Don't take those messages seriously. Many of the Internet users are below (sometimes well below) 18 years of age, and find it easy to make threats because they believe no one will ever know who they are (which is sometimes true).

The Online Business as a Conventional Business

The fact that no actual geographical location exists for an online business (except for a few megabytes of storage space on a server service's computer) has induced a few online entrepreneurs to believe that an online business is not a "real business". "The Internet is the twentieth century's version of the wild west," they say, "and there are no laws to be observed."

This would be true if their geographical address were a remote private island somewhere in the Pacific. As it is, you must obey the laws of the country you reside in. In the eyes of the law, an online business is a business, period. As long as your office/residence is located within the U.S., for instance, your online business will pay taxes there. If you sell merchandise to the residents of your own state, they would probably have to pay sales tax according to the local rate. You can be held liable for your merchandise or services and be sued as a conventional business would be. Some of the expenses conventional businesses often have to meet apply equally to online businesses: bank fees, CPA services, lawyers.

Unless you already have one, you must set up a business entity under which to conduct your business activities. This can be a corporation, sole proprietorship or a partnership. Such entity will allow you to open a bank account in the business' name, set up an account with credit card processing services, claim deductions for tax purposes, etcetera.

Other regulations which would normally apply to certain types of businesses will apply to their online counterparts as well. If you want to sell alcoholic beverages online, for instance, you will have to get a permit. Business activities which are normally prohibited, such as gambling, are equally illegal online. You may find such businesses on the Internet, but you can be certain that they are not run from the U.S. or from most other developed countries.

So — while the online world is free of regulations and central control in theory, you are still bound by the laws of the country from which you operate.

Main Types of Online Businesses

Almost all online businesses fall under at least one of the following categories:

Online Retailers. These are the virtual shops, the online vendors. What online vendors sell varies from flowers to software, and in this they are no different from the equivalent conventional retailers. They sell their products as is, and for them the Internet is just an electronic form of a storefront. The process is very similar to catalog orders via telephone — the customer visits the site, selects the item she wants, pays, and the product is sent by mail.

Only a few of the business ideas described in section II of this book deal with this category of businesses for two reasons:

A. This category of businesses needs little explaining.

B. Listing all the products you can sell on the Internet would fill several books.

Businesses that sell products online can be combined, as would be discussed in later chapters, with many other types of online businesses. Almost any type of online business can choose to sell products online in addition to their main service. For instance, if you are running a pet information center and your income is based on veterinary advice, your site can still display a few pet-related items for sale: books, muzzles, collars, powders, etcetera. You are probably more likely to sell these items than a regular online vendor who deals only with retail.

Online businesses that sell custom made products. Unlike most businesses of the first category, businesses that sell custom made items exploit the full range of Internet features and interactivity. If a customer buys a custom imprinted T-shirt online, for instance, he or she will use the Internet to view and choose from a variety of graphic designs and shirt colors, and the shirt will be printed as the customer designed it. This gives the customer instant gratification even before the products he ordered arrive by mail.

Operating a business of this category has more advantages:

➤ The ability to be unique. Customers can easily find T-shirts at their neighborhood clothing store, but only at your Internet site can they find *your own* particular line of custom designs. Internet businesses of this category are not merely substitutes for or extensions of a conventional business — they are something the customer can find *only* on the Internet. True — the same service can be offered by a mail order business, but the speed, interactivity and instant gratification are just not there for the potential customer, who will probably prefer to order the custom made T-shirt online.

➤ Small inventory. Unlike most retailers, the businesses in this category specialize in just one or two lines of products.

➤ Less competition. Businesses of this category are idea/talent based. Your competitors will try to compete in the quality or freshness of ideas, but probably not in the price. The profit margin will therefore remain relatively high.

➤ Creativity. Operating a business of this category is more interesting than operating a pure retail business, and it offers a creative challenge, the opportunity to change and reinvent yourself as you go, and the potential of coming up with "the idea of the century" some day. It is certainly more fun than being a merchant or a middleman, and it will allow you to welcome every new working day with enthusiasm and vigor.

Online businesses that sell information. These businesses, too, make use of all Internet features. The customer browses through several packages of information that are available on your site, and selects the one he wants. In most cases, once payment is settled, the information can be viewed or downloaded at once, eliminating any waiting time. For example, let's assume that a customer wants to make a will. He visits a site dedicated to the subject, and selects from the menu the appropriate will package, which will include information and a few forms that the customer can print and fill out. He pays the site, then downloads the information package right away or requests that it be sent to him immediately via e-mail.

Advantages for the business operator:

   A. No inventory whatsoever.

   B. No shipping and handling expenses. Everything is transferred electronically. Sending a thousand information packages will cost the same as sending just one.

Brokerage and referral services also fall under this category. The information they sell is only paid for if it leads to certain business transactions (e.g., the selling of a house).

Online consultation services. These are online businesses with a human touch. Here, unlike any other category of Internet businesses, the machines cannot do all the work for you. You will have to deal with your customers personally. For example, suppose that an amateur horticulturist finds out that his orchids are dying out due to an unknown reason. He contacts an online gardening center, and there he is given two options: send and receive information through e-mail, or use a chat program to discuss his problem online. Chat programs can be either vocal or text-based, and as an integral component of the Internet they are free of telephone charges (save those for local calls to the Internet server) even if the participants are continents away.

Online businesses that sell services. Here, the final product (usually information) may be sent via the Internet or hard (land) mail, but the online business will also perform some work for the consumer. Such businesses can be divided into two groups:

1. Conventional service companies. The presence of most of these businesses on the Internet bears resemblance to an iceberg — they are mostly based in the conventional business world and only their tip is visible to the online users. For this reason, some of them have only a local appeal: CPAs, computer repair services, and even Internet service providers.

2. Online service companies. No contact between the client and the server is necessary beyond that which the Internet provides. Such businesses include speech writers, editors, and of course home page designers.

Online businesses that derive their income from advertising fees. The field of possibilities open for these businesses is probably unparalleled by any other category of business. Anything goes — every idea, design, concept or presentation — as long as it pulls in the masses and records as many hits (visits to an online site) as possible. On such sites visitors can find information, entertainment, FAQ's (Frequently Asked Questions), lists about any subject, guidance, links to other sites, audio files, video files, free software and many more features. All these businesses have two things in common:

A. The main services they offer are free.

B. They hope to attract as many visitors as possible to their site, since their advertising rates depend on the number of hits they record. Advertisers rely on independent Internet evaluation and measurement companies, such as I/PRO (http://quantum.ipro.com) who works together with Nielsen Media Research, or PC-Meter (http://www.npd.com) for such statistics.

Some of the greatest online success stories fall under this category. Yahoo and the other search engines, popular chat programs such as Freetel, news or magazine sites such as MSNBC, and many others. Internet surfers would rarely agree to pay for entering a site, and would purchase products and services online only if they need or want them, but when it comes to visiting a free site that offers free information or services — well, that's what they logged on to the Internet for! They will enter your site willingly, spend not one cent while there, and will still make you money! Of all online business categories, this one seemed to have found the golden path between blending in with the Internet community and making money from it. These businesses do not ask the customers to buy, subscribe or otherwise pay for what they get, and thus they are becoming an essential part of what the Internet was originally designed for — free exchange of information between users.

When operating this kind of business, keep the following in mind:

A. Visitors will understand and accept the fact that your site carries advertisements — this is the thing that allows them to enjoy your services free of charge — but they do not want to run into a billboard whenever they visit your site. Don't make the ads on your site too large or conspicuous. Surf the Internet and you will discover that most ads are confined to narrow bars on top or at the bottom of Internet sites. Sometimes a small advertisement frame will appear near the body of the text (usually with some relevancy to it), but that is all.

B. You may, of course, sell some products or services in addition to the free information or services you offer on your site. Do not forget, however, that this would be your *secondary* business. If your site is set up only to promote the products/services you sell, then this is no free site, and the number of visitors will probably drop in proportion to the site's commercialism. Products or services for sale should compose only one option out of many on your site, and should never be presented as a condition for further free enjoyment of it.

C. Although this is not a rule of thumb, any advertising you accept on your site should complement its subject matter. If your site is a motorcycling center, for instance, your visitors may welcome advertisements that sell bike accessories, and may even come to regard them as an important feature of your site. Not only do such relevant ads not alienate the visitors to this site — they may even be counted in its favor.

probably wonder why the subject was brought up in the first place — won't the advertisers themselves be looking for such connection between the items they sell and the subject matter of the site they want to display them on? In most cases this is the case, but not always. Surf the Internet and you will be astonished at the amount of irrelevant advertising you will find there. Ads that promote get-rich-quick schemes or even legitimate services and products seem to be scattered all around the net without any logic. Such ads will serve only to alienate visitors, who would view the site as a cheap, over-commercialized hook aimed at getting them to spend money.

Try to preserve the integrity of your site as much as you can. The pro-free-information-exchange hard core of the Internet community will love you for it. However, the laws of supply and demand supersede the above, and one day you may find yourself having to choose between accepting irrelevant ads for display, and going out of business.

Online sites that sell subscriptions. The customer pays a fee and receives a password that allows him to spend a certain amount of time in the Internet site. While there, he can view information, pictures, art, listen to sound files, etcetera. You should avoid this concept unless you are absolutely sure that the features on your site are irresistible. It does not go well with the Internet's mentality.

Promotional sites. The businesses in this category are a fusion between businesses who are selling products or services (online or conventional) and free information sites. These sites do not try to sell their items directly, but have the goal of educating consumers instead. Most large corporations maintain such sites, which display their products and allow the visitor access to information, pictures, or even technical support. GM, for instance, knows that the chances of anyone buying a new car on the Internet are remote, but that displaying the features of the new models will help the consumers decide in favor of purchasing one of them. As a small entrepreneur, this category is not relevant to you unless you have reached an agreement with a large manufacturer who will pay you for your services.

Your Place in the Online Market

Define your own place in the online market by asking yourself the following questions:

1. Who is your customer? Is he a senior citizen? A teenager? A golf player? A tourist? And then, of course, the most important question of all: *is he on the Internet?*

Some consumer groups have a larger proportional representation on the Internet than others — students, for instance. Some groups have a small online representation — senior citizens, the visually impaired, people who speak little English (foreign languages sites on the Internet are relatively few, and even foreign Internet users will find that their browsing capabilities are extremely limited if they do not understand English). If you are thinking of appealing to these low-online-presence groups, your Internet business might fare worse than its conventional counterpart. If you are offering online legal advice for immigrants from under-developed countries, for example, you may waste your life away waiting for any customers to come to your online site — they simply don't have Internet access. An online student-loan broker, on the other hand, may find the Internet an excellent tool to reach potential costumers.

2. What are you going to sell? Some products sell well online: software, books, vacation packages/info, CDs, hardware, Internet services and consultation. Conversely, some items make a poor choice for online storefronts to carry: hot dogs, fresh pastry, very large items, etcetera. If you are planning to sell these, the Internet is not the place for you.

3. Is yours going to be a short term or a long term investment? If the online market for your products is still relatively small and you can't hope to make money in the near future, plan accordingly. Penny-pinch through your long wait for success. Find ways to maintain the maximum size of Internet presence with minimum amounts of money, and stick to it. If, on the other hand, you know that your online business will find customers in a very short time, and you don't have to wait for a new market to be created, you can spend more on promotion and advertising in the short run.

4. Can you pull this off? Make a business plan. Can you afford the start-up and maintenance expenses? Can you afford the time commitment? It is not hard to find an online business that will not require you to quit your day job, but even then you will still have to find the several hours a week it takes to maintain, promote and run your online business. When considering the expenses, do not forget to take into account a period of between six months and a year in which you will have no net income from your online business. Such breathing space is necessary for any new business, online or off-line.

If the business does not take too much of your time (and most online businesses should not) consider taking at least a part time job to pull you through the difficult initial days.

5. How well do you know the Internet? Before you contemplate any business decision and plan your future Internet venture, you should surf the net for as many hours as you can. Visit various commercial and non commercial sites. Develop an overall view of the Internet world and the presence of your potential customers there. With a click of a button you can scan for competitors and learn what they offer, or don't offer, their clients. You may find that a few hours' surf have caused you to change directions and decide on an altogether different type of business than you first had in mind. Don't overlook newsgroups — these can give you a pretty accurate view of the Internet population's attitude towards the products you are about to offer, your competitors, the different methods of payment online, and future developments in the market. If your aim, for example, was to sell information concerning a certain tax law, you might discover that this kind of information is distributed online free of charge and your chances of getting paid for it, therefore, are remote.

CHAPTER 2

THE ONLINE WORLD: BASICS

Origins

The Internet was created in the name of national security. Its aim was to ensure good communications between high-level government/military personnel even in the event of a nuclear war. The then existing communication system depended on the perfect working conditions of nearly all its component to successfully pass a message from one end to another. The message had to go through several designated switchboards and relays before it could reach its final destination. If one of the operators or switchboards along this route ceased to function, the communication channel would have been disrupted.

To prepare for such inevitability, a new communication system was devised. The new system would not establish a communication channel first and *then* send a message (as is the case when you dial someone's phone number and *then* talk to them), but rather the opposite — the message itself was to establish its own flexible route to its destination. The new transfer method is called *packet switching*.

Packet Switching

Packet switching means the breaking down of the transferred data into a number of small bundles of data (bytes) that would travel independently from each other. Each of these independent packets carries with it the address of its destination, the address of its source, and its own sequence information (its "place in the line"). Each packet may take different routes, utilizing the best connections available at that particular moment between its current location and its destination. On its way to its destination it passes through a number of stations, or packet switches that, according to the information on the packet itself and the switches' knowledge of the current best routes, channels it to the next switch. This process is repeated until the packet arrives at its final destination. Once there, the sequence information it carries tells the receiving computer to connect it to the other packets of the same message in the right order, and the message is reassembled.

This independent, fragmented travel assures that the packets would always find a way to their destination — even if some of the communication channels are down. This is not unlike an envelope that you send through the mail. The envelope carries its destination address, and no matter which post office it winds up at, someone there will be able to read it and send it to the next routing center (another post office).

What exactly are these switches that deal with the actual routing of packets on the Internet? These are the *routers*, high speed computers with an ability to find the best routes to send data through.

Networks and Connections

Understanding Networks is central to understanding the Internet. A network is two or more computers connected to each other for the transfer of data. Computer data, whether its final form be text, graphic, audio or video files, is based on binary data — the breaking down of information into a series of 0's and 1's. When two computers need to communicate, this binary data is being transferred across the communication lines between them. High-tech connections can handle this binary, or digital, data flow, but most Internet users have access only to ordinary telephone lines. Such lines are not designed to handle digital communication. These conventional (voice) telephone lines, through which much of the Internet's data flow is being directed, can handle only analog data — electric signals with varying frequencies. The digital data must be converted into analog data before it can be transmitted via telephone lines.

This is where the modem comes in. A modem is a device that converts digital data to analog data and vice versa. In other words, it will change the frequency of the electric signals that are sent over ordinary telephone lines in a way that will allow the modem on the other end to view them as 0's and 1's. In this way, we can connect to the Internet through conventional telephone lines. Modems vary in speed. A 28,800 bps (Bytes Per Second) modem will take one minute to send a message that a 14,400 bps modem would take two minutes to send.

Networks allow computers to exchange data among themselves, and this data moves along fast high-tech digital lines or slower telephone lines. The Internet can be thought of as one huge network, but in reality it is composed of hundreds and thousands of smaller, interconnected networks. These networks fall into one of these two categories:

A. LANs (Local Area Network). These are usually small networks that belong to small corporations or Internet sites. All the computers connected to a LAN are usually located within the same building.

B. WANs (Wide Area Networks). These networks spread over long distances, and may even span several countries. They can include LANS as well as individual computers.

The Internet connect LANs, WANs and individual computers. Routers are used to transfer data between those networks, which sometimes differ in design and working modes. The one thing all these networks and computers have in common is *TCP/IP protocol.*

Protocols are sets of rules used by computers to transfer and arrange data. For two computers to understand each other, they must use the same protocol. TCP/IP (Transport Control Protocol/Internet Protocol) is the standard protocol of the Internet, and for a computer to connect to the Internet it must use TCP/IP. TCP/IP is included in UNIX — the Internet's operating system (UNIX to the Internet is what DOS is to PCs).

The Internet is composed of the following networks:

➤ Main networks. These are the backbone of the Internet. They are composed of high speed computers that are capable of handling enormous amounts of data flow. Most of them belong to the federal government, military and defense organizations, and research institutes. The best known backbone network is that of the National Science Foundation. These organizations may be regarded as the caretakers of the Internet.

➤ Commercial networks. These include businesses with a direct connection to the Internet.

➤ Service providers. These are commercial networks that connect individual users to the Internet.

➤ Other, non commercial networks that connect to the backbone networks. These belong to regional institutes, organizations, educational institutes, foreign governments, etcetera.

➤ Independent networks with a gateway to the Internet. These include such online services as CompuServe, America Online and Prodigy. Some allow their users to communicate with the Internet, but they are not an integral part of it and have their own inner circle of subscribers.

Individual users are usually connected to the Internet via commercial service providers. For these individual users (or clients) the telephone connection to the commercial service provider is the only physical connection they need. The client connects to the service provider, and the service provider routes all outgoing and incoming messages between the client and the Internet. If, as is usually the case, the service provider is located within the same area code as the client, any call to the Internet will always be a local call — even if the person you connect to through the Internet is located in Antarctica.

Figure 2-1   The structure of the Internet.

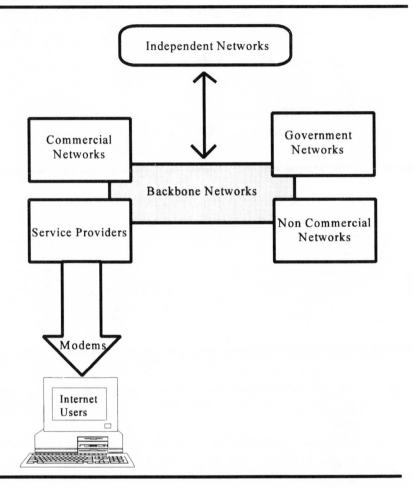

Client/Server Relations

A client on the Internet is anyone who has the ability to communicate
with host computers that use TCP/IP protocol. In other words, anyone
who logs on to the Internet is a client.

A server (host) on the Internet has a presence online. This presence
can be a virtual storefront or any other Internet site, and through it the
server can distribute information. Businesses on the Internet are servers.

Visitors to their sites are clients. Servers have an online site — allowing clients to visit them there; clients have only an e-mail address to which messages can be sent.

Every Internet server and every client with an e-mail address have a basic IP address. It is a series of four numbers that may look like this: 234.56.865.2. This combination of digits tells the packet switches where to send the data (packets).

Naturally, these IP addresses are not easy to remember, and they do not allow Internet clients to reach a site or an e-mail address by its owner's name. In addition, IP addresses change whenever a site is to move to a new online location (computer), therefore making all previous advertising and references to this address unusable. Just try to imagine listing your business in the Yellow Pages under its phone number only:

345-6765 — auto mechanic.

Not only would it make it very difficult for people to remember your business name (345-6765), but you will lose all your customers once you move to a different street and your telephone number changes. If, however, your Yellow Pages listing was to read:

Albert Green — auto mechanic — 345-6765

your customers will be able to find you no matter how many times your phone number changes. They look up your name, not your (temporary) phone number.

The Domain Name System does the same for Internet addresses. If you are looking for a virtual storefront by the domain name of WWW.GLASSFISH.COM, you need only to type this address. The numeric IP address does not concern you — it may change every day for all you care. The Internet will automatically assign those IP addresses to the domain name you have typed.

The domain name will vary in form according to the online feature the addressee is using (e-mail, World Wide Web, Gopher). The specific forms of domain names used for every feature are described in the following pages.

Summary:

A typical online communication process would look like this:

A client using a computer with a TCP/IP protocol wants to visit an online travel agency. The client keys in the travel agency's domain name. This message is being broken into data packets that travel independently to an Internet name-server computer that tells the packets what the numeric IP address of the desired domain name is, and sends them there through a series of switches. The packets are being put together by the receiving computer, which reconstructs the original message according to the sequencing information each of the packets carry. Now the receiving computer (the travel agency's site) sends a message back to the client. This message is also being broken into packets that travel independently and are put together by the client's computer. The client now has a view of the travel agency's Internet site (the message it has sent back) on his monitor.

The only physical contact the client used was the phone line between his computer and the service provider that connects him to the Internet. In other words: even if the travel agency he visited is located in another country, the client is paying only for a local call. This advantage of the Internet over ordinary telephone connections is one of the main innovations that made it the ultimate communication tool it has become.

The Main Internet Features

Most of the data flow on the Internet is channeled through five main online features: e-mail, FTP, newsgroups, Gopher and the World Wide Web. Their importance to you as an entrepreneur will be explained in detail in chapter 4, but a short introduction to these five tools is necessary to understand the full versatility of the Internet.

E-mail

E-mail is the most basic, and still most widely used, feature of the Internet. If you have an account with even the most primitive Internet service provider, you have access to e-mail service. E-mail was originally developed as a tool for exchanging text messages between users, and this has remained its chief use today. Online, text is transferred in a language named ASCII (pronounced "as-key"), which assigns a binary 7-bit numerical combination for every letter of the alphabet and for punctuation marks.

E-mail has become an acceptable form of business communication that threatens to replace most conventional tools: the post office, the telephone and the fax. In addition to text, Internet access software today allow you to attach files (such as pictures or video images) to basic e-mail messages, thus turning e-mail into a multimedia communication tool.

If you have access to e-mail, you have your own e-mail mailbox. Any messages sent to you will be kept by your mailbox (located on your Internet e-mail server's computers) until you log-in (connect) and retrieve these messages. Each mailbox has its own address, which looks like this:

george@tfinet.com (pronounced George at TFInet dot com)

The name *george* is the name of the individual (or business) you want to reach. To the right of the @ sign is the domain name — where to find him. The domain name in this case consists of *tfinet,* the name of the computer that is connected to the Internet (in this case a commercial Internet provider) and the zone name *com.* Zone names identify the nature of the addressee:

com   commercial organization

edu   educational organization

mil   military

gov   government

org   non-profit and research organizations

net   network administration and service organization

int   international organizations

Foreign countries list the country code at the top level of the domain name (usually this does not apply to U.S. servers). For example:

jerry@accting.ptbac.net.uk

This addressee in this example is Jerry, who works in the accounting division at a company named PTBAC, which is located in the UK.

FTP

FTP (File Transfer Protocol) is a program that allows the transfer of computer files across the Internet. Such files can contain images, video clips, sound recordings, software and even text arranged in a graphic form (for example, forms and documents). When users reach an FTP site, they download the files that are stored in that site, and may view or save them to their own hard disk. Public FTP sites, which allow everyone to share their files, are called *anonymous FTP*. A typical FTP address looks like this:

http://ftp.bradley.edu

Newsgroups

You may think of newsgroups (originally named USENET newsgroups) as a kind of e-mail billboard. Messages from different Internet users are sent there, rather than to other users, and can be viewed by anyone who connects to the newsgroup server. There are thousands of active newsgroups, and each is dedicated to a specific discussion topic of its own. For example: alt.agriculture.fruit or alt.drugs.caffeine

Anyone with access to a news server (most commercial Internet providers offer this option) can post messages to newsgroups. Postings are usually sent as plain text, but it is possible to post files: pictures, video clips, sound files. Posted messages remain on the newsgroup only for a few days, and then they expire.

The most common newsgroup categories are:

alt	Alternative. These newsgroups don't belong to any other category, and may range from the weird to the offensive.
bionet	Biology.
biz	Business.
comp	Computers.
k12	Teachers newsgroups (kindergarten to 12th grade)
misc	Miscellaneous subjects — sometimes a combination of several subjects within the same newsgroup.
news	Newsgroups dealing with USENET newsgroups as well as other news medium.
rec	Recreational activities.
sci	Science.
soc	Social issues.
talk	Ongoing newsgroup conversations and debates — text messages only.

Gopher

You may consider Gopher to be not so much an Internet feature by itself as a menu for other features. It is simply a menu page that allows you to select from and click on several items. Each of these items leads to an online service (for example FTP), which may belong to this or a different site. The items on the Gopher's menu appear as plain text, but clicking on them may send any of a variety of Internet commands: file transfers, database searches, linking to other sites or menus, etcetera.

Figure 2-2   A typical Gopher site

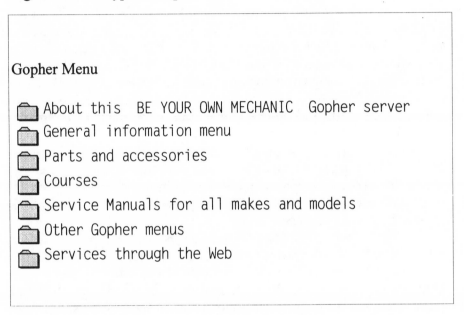

Gopher Menu

📁 About this BE YOUR OWN MECHANIC Gopher server
📁 General information menu
📁 Parts and accessories
📁 Courses
📁 Service Manuals for all makes and models
📁 Other Gopher menus
📁 Services through the Web

A Gopher can act as a virtual storefront. If such is the case, the menu will display various items or services for sale, or any related information. Most Gopher sites are maintained by universities and research institutes, and have been set up to provide multiple solutions (files, documents, databases) for information seekers, and concentrate them in one site. A typical Gopher address is: yaleinfo.yale.edu.   You can reach Gopherspace through TELNET services such as gopher.virginia.edu or gopher://gopher.ncc.go.jp/ .

You can search Gopherspace through:

> http://galaxy.einet.net/gopher/gopher.html   (Galaxy)

The World Wide Web

The difference between the World Wide Web (a.k.a. WWW or *the Web*) and Gopher can be compared to the difference between visiting a house and looking at its blue prints. Unlike Gopher, the Web allows site creators to enhance their online presence with graphics. Not only can pictures and graphics be put into a Web site, but even the entire background can be created in different patterns and colors. Instead of selecting and clicking on an item in a menu (as in Gopher), the Web user can click on a picture, icon or text and be transferred to the desired Web page or feature. Any picture or text that sends a command to the Internet when clicked on is called a "hot-key." When the hot-key is text, this text (known as *hypertext*) is highlighted in a different color from the rest of the text. These hypertext are located within the body of the text, and they change the appearance of a typical Web page from the linear Gopher-like menu system to a new, flexible form of presentation, which is a fertile ground for a creative person.

A Web site consists of one or more pages. The first page, to which most visitors to the site arrive first, is called the home page. This home page may be designed to look like a menu or it may take some other shapes and forms. If the Web site has more than one page, the home page will allow the visitors access to the other pages. For example, the home page of an online storefront will display general information about the company, and allow the visitors to select and view information and pictures of individual products (displayed on other pages of the site).

The endless possibilities enabled by the Web have made it the most interesting, fast growing, talked-about feature of the Internet. You may have seen very few news reports covering FTP or Gopher sites, but when it comes to the WWW, every medium-to-large size corporation who opens up a Web site receives maximum coverage. Why? Because it looks good on the TV screen. So excessive is this media coverage of the Web that a large population has come to believe that the Internet and the Web are the same thing, and that nothing else exists online.

With all its possibilities and promises, however, the Web has one serious flaw — speed. A much larger amount of data is needed to transfer images than is needed for plain text. As a result, pictures and graphics take longer to download. Web pages may be graphically attractive, but usually require some patience on behalf of the viewer. The speed of the modem the visitor to a Web site uses is definitely a factor in determining the time it will take him to view it. However, even with the fastest modems, some Web pages may take a minute or more to fully appear on the user's screen. For this reason, a good Web site will include plain text as well as graphics, and may even give users the option to sort through text documents without the delaying effects of the attached images.

Even with its shortcomings, the WWW seems to be the future of the online world. The media hype has pushed many corporations to set up a presence on the Web, and many users to surf it. Even devout Web haters often find themselves using it, since an increasing number of services and online information centers can be found only there. As the first wave of overproduced Web sites ebbs away, new Web sites are learning how to make better use of text and how to improve on the speed of downloading. The majority of Internet users are not computer buffs, and surfing text-only, dull looking sites does not appeal to them. As the number of Internet users grow, so will the percentage of this latter group, and the use of the Web will grow in proportion to the other Internet features. In addition, the near future may see a growing number of users connect to the Internet through digital cables, TV cables or DSL technology, all of which are hundreds of times faster than modems.

Another important consideration in favor of Web sites is their appeal to advertisers. With the exception of a few unsolicited messages sent out to newsgroups and private e-mail addresses, advertisers are probably going to concentrate *only* on Web sites. There are two reasons for this:

1. Ads are almost always of a graphic nature, and so is the Web.

2. The Web gets all the media coverage. Survey people without Internet access, or those who are not computer literate, and you will find that most of them accept the picture of the online world as the media paints it for them — that the Web is the only game in town. So who wouldn't want to jump on the band wagon?

This notwithstanding, an Internet entrepreneur must never overlook the Internet's other tools, such as auto-responders (see pages 49-50), which in some cases are just as important to the success of an online business as a Web site is. E-mail and newsgroups are here to stay even if the Web's share increases dramatically.

Figure 2-3   A typical Web site

How to save hundreds of dollars a year in car maintenance and repair costs.

You and your car: an overview
General information about car maintenance and repair

Buying parts and accessories
Where to look for them

Courses

Service manuals
All makes and models

Links
Find Similar sites

Articles

Contact us

For Internet users to be able to enjoy the full spectrum of the Web, their computers must use a client software such as Netscape Navigator. These software, better known as Web browsers, can easily be downloaded free of charge from their creators' sites as well as from many other sites on the Internet that have agreed to distribute them.

A very important feature of the Web is the ability to support forms. A virtual form, just as its conventional counterpart, allows the user to key in her name, address and credit card information, among other data. Visitors to commercial Web sites can thus order products on the spot, without the need to go back and forth between e-mail services and Web or FTP pages. Web site addresses (a.k.a URLs) look like this:

http://www.amazon.com

However, keep in mind that some Web sites do not have the prefix: www before their URL.

Less Common Internet Features

Mailing Lists are similar to newsgroups, with the exception that you have to subscribe to them in order to read them, and that the articles are then sent directly to your e-mail address. One well known mailing list program is ListServe (short for List Service). Whenever a message is posted to a ListServe group, it is received by all subscribers. Some mailing lists (as well as some newsgroups) are moderated — that is, someone sorts out the incoming e-mail messages and decides which ones to post for the subscriber's view.

WAIS (Wide Area Information Servers). This is a program that searches a word or a string of letters in a certain database (not unlike the Window's "find" command). WAIS is usually incorporated into other features such as Web sites, and the user is often unaware of its being a separate tool. It is a very important addition to sites that hold vast amounts of text, or to commercial sites with a great number of items for sale. For example, an online bookstore with a huge inventory may want to incorporate a WAIS tool into its Web site to help customers locate a certain title or to find an author's name.

There are also independent WAIS sites on the Internet, which offer access to general databases.

Telnet. The Telnet protocol is an online remote control. It allows the users to control a computer they are connected to as if they were working that computer's keyboard. Telnet is used to allow visitors to a certain site (the remote computer) to search, retrieve, and view files, and to perform many other tasks with the files located on the remote computer. Telnet is usually combined with other features, and is rarely presented as an independent service.

Archie. Archies (short for archive) are lists of file names from FTP sites. It is basically a file-search service that allows users to find the location of the desired file by entering its name.

Finger. This is a command that allows you to view some basic information on businesses and individuals who have chosen to store this information in a special text file (named *.plan* or *.project*). The finger command will only work, therefore, with some e-mail addresses. The information displayed by this command may vary from telephone numbers to a price list, as well as the person's last log-in (the last time he viewed his e-mail messages). Not every system supports finger, but you can always use services like Yahoo's list of finger gateways to view some of them.

Veronica. A file search service similar to Archie, with the exception that Veronica searches Gopher menus rather than FTP sites.

Chat programs allow you to converse in real time with other users by using either text or vocal communications. You can carry a telephone style conversation with someone from Japan, for example, and be charged only for the local connection to your Internet server.

Don't let the variety of Internet features overwhelm you — most Internet users today are not computer buffs, and they use only three main tools: e-mail, the Web, and newsgroups.

The Online World Outside the Internet

As you probably know, the Internet is not synonymous with the online world. Not every service or computer we can reach with a modem or even through the Internet itself is an integral part of the Internet. Some online systems do not belong to the main backbone networks that make the Internet, or even to its smaller components. Those independent systems, however, *are* part of the online world, and many have access to the Internet. Some of them are small single PCs while others are huge networks and online communities unto themselves.

BBS

BBS stands for Bulletin Board System. A BBS can be defined as any computer that has the following characteristics:

1. It is connected to a telephone line through a modem.

2. It allows callers to use its software and files.

BBSs are usually single computers, as opposed to large, multi-computer networks. A BBS might be similar in content and presentation to an ordinary Internet site, but clients would have to dial the BBS's phone number in order to reach it, because the BBS is not directly connected to the Internet (although a few can be reached through the Internet).

Independent Networks:

Independent networks include: CompuServe, Delphi, GEnie, Prodigy and America Online. These independent networks are online communities in their own right. Some have their own online malls, magazines and just about every other service the Internet may provide. However, the amount of resources that are normally available to Internet users cannot be matched by these networks. CompuServe, Delphi and GEnie were originally text based networks, but as things change fast in the online world, most of them now offer a large variety of online features. Internet access policy varies from network to network, but most now offer unlimited Internet access to their subscribers.

The networks that support graphics, such as Prodigy and America Online, have one distinct advantage over the Web, the Internet's graphical equivalent: while a visitor to a Web site must download a tremendous volume of data in order to display images, America Online or Prodigy subscribers use a special software sent to them by these services, which has the images already stored within it. Instead of complete graphic images, these subscribers need only to download short instructions for their computers, which will then place images (from their image library) in the right places on the screen. As a result, the transfer speed of images is much higher than that of the Web, and graphics appear almost instantaneously on the user's screen. The trade off, of course, is the small graphic variety — only a certain number of image combinations can be offered by the independent networks' software, and constant updates are required to allow for new images to be seen. Of course, most independent networks' subscribers can choose between using the network's services and logging on to the Internet (through the network).

CHAPTER 3

YOUR SERVER PRESENCE

To do business on the Internet, you must first set up a server. Your server, or Internet site, will provide clients with information, resources or other online services. Your connection to the online world as a server is different from the basic dial-up connection clients use. A client's dial-up account, which connects to the Internet through a modem, has no presence on the Internet except for an e-mail box. This e-mail box, or e-mail address, exists somewhere on the service provider's computers, and the user can download all incoming mail once he logs in to it. The protocol used for this storing and retrieving of e-mail messages is called POP3 (Post Office Protocol 3).

Internet sites, or servers, have a much larger, more complex online presence than clients. However, your server, whether a Web site or a Gopher site, is physically no more than a certain amount of digital data that is stored on someone's computer and can be reached by clients 24 hours a day. The question for you, the entrepreneur, is: on whose computer will you store your site? In other words — how will your site connect to the Internet?

There are four options: a direct (dedicated) connection to the Internet; setting up an account with a server service; renting a space in an online mall; or setting up an account with a non-Internet network (Prodigy, America Online).

Connecting Directly to the Internet

Connecting directly to the main networks of the Internet (which can also be done through a server service) allows for speedy data transfer and better control of your site. However, it requires a UNIX workstation, a dedicated connection and a leased digital line. The initial investment in equipment alone would be $10,000 or more. In addition, unless you know a great deal of UNIX (the operating system of the Internet), you will have to hire professionals to set up the whole system for you — computers, routers, CSU/DSU (the digital equivalent of a modem), interface cards, firewalls (security systems) and software. Professional help can easily mount up to several thousands dollars. Monthly costs for leased lines (such as the high speed T3, T1 or slower 19-128kbps lines) vary, but they are substantial and can easily reach several hundred dollars a month.

These expenses might prove economical for large, high traffic sites. Their online expenses would be high anyway due to the high volume of Internet traffic in their sites — even if they choose to use a server service instead of a direct connection. Small businesses, on the other hand, do not require this expensive type of Internet connection. Unless you believe that the type of business you are planning requires such a dedicated connection, you are better off setting up shop on someone else's already established hardware.

Using a Server Service

Your site, which as previously explained is physically no more than a certain number of bytes clumped up together in a storage space, does not have to be stored in your own computer. You can rent the space needed for storing your virtual shop from a server service. The server service takes care of everything that a direct Internet connection would require you to purchase: the computers, routers, high speed connections to the Internet and the hassle of putting it all together to work.

Server services are not unlike car pools: they allow servers to share the expenses of maintaining a connection to the Internet with other servers. Many of the service providers (by which clients' dial up IP accounts are set up) also offer server services. See page 297 for a list of some of the many server services you can find in the U.S.

You can ask your server service to establish a virtual server presence. This means that your domain name will look like this: www.yourname.com. Visitors to a virtual server will not be able to tell by its address, appearance or features whether this site is directly connected to the Internet or located on a server service's computer. Online, all businesses can be equal — your next door neighbor can set up an Internet site with the same size and features as any site GM might open. There is no advantage, therefore, to a direct Internet connection over a connection through a server service as far as site appearance goes, and both allow you to offer your customers the same features and services. A direct connection should be considered only if you anticipate a huge number of hits (several hundred thousands a day). A large online mall, for example, may wish to choose this type of connection.

How to choose the right server service for your online business? What should you expect from a server service? This depends mostly on the type of Internet business you wish to run. Is it going to be a Web site? A Gopher site? Are you going to allow your customers to place orders online? Do you want to give them the option of e-mailing you their comments?

Other points worth considering when comparing server services:

➤ Is there a set up fee in addition to the monthly fee? A set up fee should be no more than twice the monthly fee.

➤ Is there a flat monthly fee or does it depend on the number of hits your site records?

➤ Do they offer free (and patient!) consultation and technical support?

➤ How will you update or change your site — can you do it online or are you required to send the server service a floppy disk containing the new files?

➤ Do they support all the tools your business needs (e.g., forms, mailbots)?

➤ Will you be charged for credit card transactions (other than charges by the credit card processing company)?

➤ What will be the size of your Internet site? Some server services' pricing structure benefit the large sites while others prove more economical for businesses with a single Web home page.

➤ Do they use high speed equipment and connections?

➤ Do they offer any help in promotion (e.g., free registration with search engines)?

➤ Are there any hidden fees (other than for setting up a domain name)? Will they charge you for updating your site? Does your basic monthly fee cover only a small server space that will force you to pay extra for additional space?

➤ Do they give you your own POP e-mail address (with your domain name)?

➤ Do they allow you to resell Web space (especially important for small malls)?

➤ Do they support credit card processing software and forms?

➤ Will they give you periodical reports on your site's usage (at least the number of hits it got)?

➤ How long have they been in business — which brings us to the more important question — how long are they going to stay in business? Keep in mind, however, that even the oldest server services are probably under five years old.

➤ Will your site be a virtual server — does it have its own domain name rather than appearing under the server service's domain name?

➤ Don't dismiss the option of setting up accounts with two server services — for example, one for your Web site and one for your e-mail auto responder. Sometimes you will find that one server service specializes in one feature, which it offers at a great price, while the rest of the package falls within the normal price range.

➤ Know in what direction your business is heading. The server service may make a few suggestions, but inexperienced servers should not be intimidated by them. The server service's staff may know all there is to know about the Internet, but they usually know little about your type of business. For example, a server service might recommend that you choose a secure server for secure credit card transactions, but if you believe that you won't have to offer such an option to your customers in the near future, this may be an unnecessary expense for you.

➤ You may want to negotiate a package deal; price quotes are rarely firm here and competition is increasing daily. As with any other service, compare the prices and services of several server services before choosing the one you want.

Setting up an online presence through a server service is a sound business decision for small businesses. The costs are kept under control, tailor made to fit your business needs, and you don't need to hire overly paid experts or to become one yourself. It allows you to make full use of all the Internet's tools and to be registered with your own domain name (see chapter 4 for more details on domain names).

Online Malls

Just like a conventional mall, an online mall provides a roof for a large number of shops. Shop owners pay the mall rent or a percentage of their gross sales. They get from the mall a place to do business and some help in attracting customers — mainly by advertising. Online malls vary greatly in the range of services they offer. Some allow Web sites; others are Gopher based; some invest heavily in promotion, others only try to attract more (competing) virtual shops to their mall. A mall may be connected either directly to the Internet or through a server service.

There are two ways to join an online mall:

1. The Internet site/virtual shop is independent, and is linked only to the mall's directory. This is a form of advertising, and the mall will charge you either a flat fee, or according to the number of users who linked to your site from the mall. You do not rent any space from the mall save the few lines that describe your business to mall visitors.

2. The Internet site/virtual shop rents a space from the online mall and establishes its online presence there. The mall becomes the virtual shop's server service, and charges accordingly. Some online malls are even known to charge a percentage of the servers' sales. The mall takes care of advertising, promoting and maintaining your site. Some may even help you design it. The mall may handle credit card transactions (an important feature for merchants who are not approved by credit card processing companies) or other forms of payment.

Is renting a space on an online mall a good idea? That depends on the mall itself. Shop around. There are two important points you should remember:

1. When a visitor stops by a conventional strip mall, he is exposed to all sorts of stores. Even if his intended goal is to purchase a pair of jeans, he is involuntarily window-shopping as he walks through the mall. In addition to the pair of jeans, this customer is likely to purchase various other items from different stores — shoes, music CDs, a magazine, etc. The same visitor to an online mall would simply use the site's directory to view *only* the (virtual) clothing stores. Impulse buys are thus reduced to a minimum.

2. A conventional mall has a physical limit to the number of shops within it. Not so an online mall. You may find that your online business has become lost among dozens of similar businesses or, if the mall has outgrown its Internet connection's capacity, lose

customers who would never reach your site because they could not connect to the mall during the busy hours.

Connecting Through Non-Internet Online Networks

Not everyone who does business on the Internet is actually located within it. Some online networks, like Prodigy or America online, allow you to set up shop with them and still offer your products or services to the entire Internet community. Often you will find that they offer the best deal for a small business that takes its first steps in the online world. Those services make the design of your site a cinch, and provide you with all the necessary services and hardware. However, there are some cons to establishing a business presence there:

> ➤ You may not have access to all the Internet tools (such as online forms for placing customers' orders), and you are limited in the services and features you can offer your customers. This might change, however, and you will probably want to contact the individual networks from time to time and inquire about changes in policy.

> ➤ Your online site may be limited in size. Again, this might change as the independent networks become more competitive and more involved with the Internet community.

BBSs are mini independent networks. They are not a part of the Internet, but some can be reached through Gophers, anonymous FTP sites, or even the Web. BBSs are normally reached by dialing their phone numbers. Establishing your presence on a BBS requires setting up a computer equipped with the right connection software and hardware. Promoting a BBS is much harder than promoting a Web site, and getting advertisers to sponsor a BBS will prove difficult. In a nut shell — BBS is not a good idea for a small business.

Chapter 4

DESIGNING AND MAINTAINING YOUR SERVER PRESENCE

Domain Name

Once you have decided to establish a server presence on the Internet, the first thing you have to do is set up a domain name for it. A domain name will allow you to move your site to another server service without having to change your online address. Domain names have to be registered with the InterNIC registration service. Previous legal registrations supersede InterNIC registration. For example, if you discover that the domain name ups.com is available and decide to use it, UPS may still be entitled to use this domain name (which you will lose), and they may even sue you for using their trade name.

To check the availability of a domain name, you can:

> Call the InterNIC at 703 742-4777 and speak to a representative.
> or:
> Go to http://rs.internic.net/cgi-bin/whois and key in the requested name. This database will tell you if this name is in use or not.

If the name you want is not used by someone else, forward it to the server service that handles your site. They will register it with the InterNIC. If you are connected directly to the Internet you will have to do this yourself and supply the InterNIC with your site's IP address (the numerical address which refers to the site's physical location and is not transferable), which they will assign to your domain name. When moving to a new physical location (computer), you or your new server service will have to notify the InterNIC of the new IP address they need to assign to your domain name. The type of domain name you will have depends, of course, on the type of Internet presence you are planning.

What Type of Server Should You Set Up?

The first concept that comes to mind whenever the term "online business" is mentioned, is the World Wide Web. A Web site is more interesting, aesthetic, and it seems more promising and futuristic in nature than any other Internet feature. As we discussed in Chapter 2, the Web's main problem is its sites' slow downloading speed. This difficulty will probably be overcome soon: at the end of the slow-Internet-connection tunnel, we can even now see the advent of cable TV as the future Internet carrier. The super fast speed of these cables will allow even the most complex Web pages to appear instantaneously on the user's screen. A new technology called DSL may do the same thing through conventional telephone lines.

However, until this happens, many other online tools should be considered as well when deciding on your Internet presence. These tools can be incorporated into a Web site or operated independently to complement your Web site's services. For certain types of businesses you may even find that setting up a Web site is totally unnecessary.

E-mail Presence

The simplest form of Internet presence is e-mail. Conducting business through e-mail can be done in one of the two following ways:

1. By answering your incoming e-mail personally. This might prove a necessity if you are handling technical questions that require individual attention. If you want to handle a high number of requests for sales info, or to answer your customers' frequently asked questions (FAQ), sending manual responses will no doubt quickly become tiresome.

2. Through auto responders. This is an efficient, labor-free way to handle a high volume of correspondence that does not require a personal touch. The mail robot, or mailbot program, sends out a standard reply to anyone who sends a message to its e-mail address. For example, let us suppose that you offer a free list of inexpensive motels throughout the U. S. The customer sends a blank e-mail message to your mailbot's e-mail address, and a few minutes later she finds the desired list in her e-mail box.

Because of their advantages, auto responders should be considered an important tool for any online business. Auto responders are capable of doing a lot more than just sending standard messages in response to blank messages. They can allow costumers to choose from several items, and then send them information accordingly. In the above example, for instance, the customer, rather than leaving the message blank, could send the mailbot the name of a state. The mailbot will send her only the names of inexpensive hotels located within that particular state. The problem with this feature is that it tends to make any advertising seem complex. Compare these two ads, the first for a simple mailbot, the second for a complex one:

1. *For a complete list of inexpensive hotels throughout the U.S.A., send a blank e-mail message to hotels@yournet.com*

2. *For a list of inexpensive hotels throughout the U.S.A., send for information to hotels@yournet.com. Include the name of any state you intend to travel to in the "subject" line, or the word "USA" if you wish to receive the full list.*

Most people with an Internet access would be able to follow these instructions, but you might lose some who run into difficulties with this command system, and especially if the auto responder is more complicated than the one in the above example. Several blank-message mailbots, each with a distinctive name that describes its content, might be more consumer-friendly than one complex auto responder.

Make sure your server does not charge you for each message your mailbot sends out. Normally, there are limitations on the maximum size of the message your mailbot can send, but as this limit would rarely be less than 4-5 pages, this should be of no concern to you. Unless you are sending long lists, customers would seldom read a longer message. The time it takes a mailbot to respond might vary from one server service to another, but it ranges from a few seconds to a few minutes.

> People who ask for information through a mailbot want just that. The reply they receive from the auto responder must be concise, to-the-point, and should never give the impression of junk mail.

Mailing lists are another feature your e-mail site can offer. They are similar in function to an auto responder, with the exception that a message (usually with the key word "subscribe") received there will prompt the mailbot to place the sender on a mailing list. Instead of one response to his message, the sender will have subscribed to a mailing service. He will receive additional messages on a regular basis from now on without the need to ask for them individually. Mailing lists fall into two categories:

1. Interactive mailing lists. These can be moderated or unmoderated, and much like newsgroups they allow subscribers to send messages that all other subscribers can view. In an unmoderated mailing list, every message sent by any subscriber would reach every other subscriber's e-mail box. In a moderated list, a central authority receives all messages and decides which to send on to the list's subscribers. For you as a business operator, moderated mailing lists can be an important tool. You can set up discussion groups for your customers, encourage exchange of information between them and answer any questions they might have. Unlike newsgroups, where users have to be active and visit the newsgroup in order to view its posted messages, mailing list messages are sent directly to the subscribers' e-mail boxes. This way, there is a smaller chance of customers drifting off and losing contact with your business.

2. Mailing lists (moderated) that send a series of messages which are generated by one entity. For example, a large film

manufacturer might use such a mailing list to send product updates and information to amateur photographers on a weekly basis.

For more information on mailing lists, see page 35.

The e-mail features discussed above can and should be incorporated into Web sites. Examples:

➤ Some Internet users (albeit few) still do not have browser capabilities — they cannot view Web pages. The reason might be that they are connected to the Internet through text-based independent networks, or that they use old computers. The only thing *all* online users have in common is e-mail, which is offered even by the most pristine networks. You can use a mailbot to allow people who have access only to text based sites to gain access to the information displayed on your Web site.

➤ Interaction. For most Web sites, the only way their visitors can make any comments or suggestions concerning the site is by sending e-mail. Visitors click on highlighted hypertext (that will usually say "write us" or "e-mail us") and automatically activate their e-mail programs, which will pop up and allow them to send you a message immediately.

➤ Processing orders. If you don't have the encryption software Web sites now use to secure credit card transactions, or if your customers are reluctant to use them, you can always use e-mail for processing orders, accepting credit card numbers, and solving customers' payments problems.

FTP Presence

Linking anonymous FTP sites to your Web or Gopher site can greatly enhance your Internet presence. Using such FTP sites, your customers can choose from a variety of files and programs to download.

Many FTP files are text files. However, unlike standard e-mail, FTP allows you to use different fonts, special features (highlighted text, bold text) or even graphics. For example, you can use FTP to send whole documents or forms to your customers. Another important use of FTP is for sending software online. For you as an online entrepreneur, there are two main categories of software that customers can download:

1. Software that allow customers to use your site. A good example of this category is online applications that allow users to view certain Web features (such as audio or video files). You may want to encourage visitors to link to an FTP site where they can download such applications and listen to audio files on your site.

2. Commercial software. These programs, whether created by you or distributed in agreement with the creators, can be distributed in one of the following ways:

   A. As prepaid software. The software is sold as any other product would be.

   B. As freeware. As the name suggest, these programs are offered free of charge by the creator, who usually hopes to make money from selling newer versions or added features, or, if the software is used online (for example, a browser), from displaying commercial advertisements on it.

   C. As shareware. You may think of these programs as being sold through a "30 days free trial" or "cash upon liking" offers. After an evaluation period, which is usually 30 to 90 days long, the customer has to decide whether to pay the creator or stop using the software.

FTP can add color to your site and make it interesting and appealing. You can use FTP to transfer media files to your customers: voice or music recordings, short video clips, or pictures. Users can save downloaded files on their hard disks, and view or hear them at will. Most FTP sites on the Internet are an integral part of Web sites and are not independent.

Gopher vs. Web Presence

Gophers allow you to combine many online services and sites and place them under the same menu. Once you have established a site in Gopherspace, your Gopher can be placed under a larger menu or directory, and Internet users can reach you from various Gopher directories. A visitor to your site can scan your menu in a glance, and decide which item to choose. This organized, clear arrangement is considered by some to be superior to the Web's hypertext or links system (which is why an increasing number of Web sites are using menus — and with icons and graphics that make them even easier to use than Gophers' menus). Gophers allow their customer a speedy retrieval of information or files, and do not confuse users with glitzy graphics or advertisements.

Web sites, which can offer the same features as Gopher sites, have two main advantages over Gophers:

1. They are more interesting, with appealing graphics, animation, color, pleasing backgrounds, and a variety of fonts. Web sites appeal to our visual sense, and it has been said that "the eyes are the tool of temptation". Contents aside, a Gopher site would always seem dull when compared to a Web site (see figures 2-2 and 2-3), and may not inspire its visitors to explore it.

2. Creativity. Although both allow creativity where content is concerned, only Web sites allow it on the presentation level. Examine magazine or TV ads. Many of them, and some of the best, say very little. Does this mean that the advertiser has nothing to say? No. It means that some creative person has found a different, visual medium to convey their message best. A Gopher site tells such a person: "I'm not going to use your genius no matter how much it is going to help me." A Web site says: "Do your best!"

Web sites have one fault, of course: speed (see pages 32-33, 48). It was predicted by several people in the computer industry that for this reason, Web sites will not become the future of online business. There are, however, some factors we have to consider before rushing to such conclusions:

1. The Internet is fast becoming a medium for the masses. Although the core of "pure" Internet and computer professionals may prefer a text-based, fast access information site, the new generation of Internet users, already the majority, is made up of ordinary people. The Web, especially if we consider the tremendous media coverage it receives, may be the only game in town for these entertainment seekers. The main chunk of the time they spend online will go to Web sites — and only rarely will they visit a Gopher or an FTP site.

2. As previously discussed, communication technology is developing fast (see pages 32-33, 48). In future, loading speeds will no longer be an issue. This "speed revolution" will probably take place within the next few years.

There are several things Web sites can do *today* to overcome the speed problem:

➤ Offer a text-only option. This feature will allow visitors to your Web site to view its content even if their browsers do not support graphics, or if they simply prefer to omit the time consuming extravagance. You can also refer such visitors to an e-mail auto responder (see pages 49-50), or to a text-only Web page which will include no graphics or HTML commands.

➤ Keep your Web site simple. Animation requires longer downloading time. So do large images or complex backgrounds. Some of the best Web pages consist of plain white backgrounds, several small images or icons, and the rest is just well typeset, eye pleasing text. These Web pages do not take long to appear on the user's screen, and appeal both to content minded users and to the new generation of Web surfers.

➤ Establish additional online presences. Many businesses and organizations offer Gophers and anonymous FTP's as well as

Web sites. Keep at least a minimal presence wherever you believe you may find customers.

Of course, not every solution is right for every type of business. Large sites, for example, will find it hard to put their entire content on an auto responder's message. Also, the text option is usually unnecessary where there are no time consuming graphics.

Check the size of your files before you publish them on the Web. Make sure these sizes are withing reason (up to 250Kb for a home page and as little as possible for other Web pages).

Bottom Line — which Feature Should You Go With?

This depends a lot on the consumer you are trying to reach. Does he have access to the Web? Does he prefer content based information centers to graphics and entertainment? Do you have a lot to say and many items to sell to him, or can you put it all in one auto responder message?

It is probably safe to say that for most businesses, a Web site will do no harm and possibly a lot of good. Future potential alone justifies such a move. However, to be on the safe side and to maximize the business potential of an Internet presence, other features should be considered as well. Some e-mail features may be combined into your Web site, and, if the need arises, a separate Gopher or mailbot should also be established (for example, if you find out that many of your customers connect to your site through text-based online services).

Above all, be flexible. Search the Internet to see how businesses similar to yours are presenting themselves online. However, make sure the sites you picked to study have been in existence for some time — online businesses constantly experiment with new designs and features.

Don't hesitate to drop a feature that has proved unpopular with your customers, or to add new features that other sites have been using successfully. Perseverance does count, however, so don't give up on your site and its design before you have spent at least several months promoting and maintaining it.

Making Your Web Site Work

If you choose a Web site for your Internet presence, read the following guidelines:

➤ Don't make your site too large. Internet users do not appreciate complex Web sites that force them to go through several Web pages in order to find the service or information they need. After visiting your site's home page, users should know exactly what your site has to offer and what to do next. Don't fill your entire home page with a lengthy description of who you are and what your life ambition is. The home page must be a menu — perhaps with small icons or hypertext, perhaps arranged in a professional, graphic way — but nevertheless a menu. If you want your customers to learn more about your company, allow them to select this information from the menu, but don't force it on them

   For example, if you sell books, your home page should present visitors with a short description of your business (how long have you been in business, what is your specialty) and, following it, the options they have: sections dealing with business books, travel books, fiction, poetry, etcetera. Once an option has been selected, the customer is transferred to a secondary page, where more specific selections can be made: search by author's name, search by book title, etcetera. The customer finds the desired book quickly, and does not waste time having to navigate through several Web pages of vague, irrelevant information.

➤ Place your commercial hook in the home page. It is the home page most potential customers are going to visit first, and it is therefore the home page's mission to keep them in your site. Your sales copy must be appealing and succinct. Lines such as "Books at half the retail price!" for instance, must be the first thing customers see when they enter your site — even before the company name.

➤ Graphics. As previously discussed, images, animation and pictures should complement your Web pages; but don't be too generous with them. Aside from slowing down the speed of your Web pages, too many graphics can alienate the visitor. An increasing number of people are tired of gimmicky Web sites, and would rather have your site's message come across clearly and succinctly.

➤ Links. Links to other Web pages can work for an online business in two ways:

1. The sites you link to agree to reciprocate, and link to your site in return, thereby sending you more visitors.

2. The links themselves add a lot to your site. They add resources to those displayed on your site, and they are a factor in creating repeat customers, who would come back to your site because sites that deal with the same subject matters can be easily reached from there. Your site becomes an information center, a reference service for online resources, rather than being just another commercial site.

For more about links, see page 73.

➤ Consider adding search engines to your site. If you offer a vast pool of information or a great number of items for sale, offer your customers a database search service to help them find the item of their choice. Incorporating such a service into your virtual book store, for example, will enable visitors to search books by author names or title.

➤ FAQ (Frequently Asked Questions). Giving visitors to your site access to FAQ files will save you a lot of e-mail correspondence and visitors' complaints. It will probably take several weeks of answering your customers questions yourself before you will be able to put together a FAQ list, but try to predict some of these questions before you even establish your site.

➤ Information. Even if your site is a virtual shop and the only thing you want to do is sell flowers, giving your customers free information is a good idea. Remember — if your site is no different from a magazine ad or a TV commercial, you lose all the advantages the Internet can give you. Unlike TV, where you are confined to 30 second spots, or magazines, which limit the amount of information you can display (within a normal advertising budget), the Internet imposes virtually no limitations on the length of the message you can convey. You can put entire manuals and catalogs online at a minimal cost, having to pay only for storage space on the computer that carries your site. The Internet community has learned to expect just that — that they will be given, should they so desire, access to tremendous pools of information.

➤ *What's new* option. This option allows repeat visitors to receive updates and view any changes or additions to your site without having to re-visit each of its pages. The time-starved Internet community appreciates such a feature very much.

➤ Change. Since your aim is to keep people coming back to your site, you will have to dedicate a considerable part of your time for this purpose, and constantly change your site. Users will rarely come back to a static site that has seen no changes or additions in the past few months or even weeks. This does not mean that you have to take important articles off your site just because they have been posted there for a few months — you still have newcomers to think of. What change does mean for your site is constantly adding new articles or items to it, and removing unimportant ones. Even if you have an online shop that specializes in just one item, you can always add new information about your product, media reviews, updated FAQ's, pictures, technical support, more links, references to additional reading material (books or magazine articles), guest articles, or even a few small gimmicks (so long as they don't upstage the main subject).

➤ Allow customers to contribute their own talents to your site. For example, if you are selling motorcycle accessories online, many of your customers will probably be more than glad to share their riding experiences and advice with other users. Not only will your site benefit from more information and advice based on first hand experience, but it will also ensure that many of your visitors will come back just for the chance you give them to donate their own material to the site.

➤ Sound. More and more Internet sites give users access to audio files in addition to text based articles. The Internet is a multimedia tool, and there is no reason to ignore your visitors' sense of hearing. Instead of reading an article about riding techniques, for instance, many people (especially young) would prefer to listen to it being read. Unlike video files, which may take a long time to download, audio files transfer relatively quickly and some can be listened to in real time (i.e. you don't have to wait for the whole file to download before the sound begins to play).

➤ Don't try to compete with the Sears catalog. Unless you display only a handful of items on your site, attaching a color photograph to every item will not be practical and will slow down the downloading speed of your site considerably. To get around this problem, some Web sites display tiny icons next to the item's text description. Clicking on these icons will take your customer to another Web page, where the full size photograph of the item appears.

➤ If you are selling products that can easily be found at any neighborhood shop, your site's main feature should be your low prices. You must offer better deals than conventional local stores do. Any other Web feature — graphics, tons of information, online help — is no substitute. They may attract many visitors to your site, but without the discount these visitors will never become buyers.

➤ If the feedback you get from your customers suggests that many of them know people who would like to use your services but who do not have Internet access, consider expanding into more conventional operations. As a rule of thumb, if you find out that your business would do better as a mail-order or a phone-order business, don't hesitate to veer to that direction. You are in it for the money and not in order to become an Internet purist.

➤ Add a "back to the home page" option on every Web page. While it is true that visitors can use their browser's own "back" command to go to the previous page, some of them will enter your site from a secondary page (through a search engine, for instance) and these visitors will have no other way of reaching your home page.

➤ Add your land address or telephone number at the bottom of your home page.

➤ For the benefit of repeat customers, include a "Last updated on..." line on your home page.

➤ Add your press release (see page 76) to the site. This will allow visiting journalists to save the time and trouble of contacting you in case they are interested in your site.

Bottom line: not every one of these guidelines is right for every Web site. Your site will have to be tailor-made to suit your potential customers. Understanding who your customer is will be the key to everything that follows: choosing the right site, planning and designing it, adding features, updating.

Should You Hire Experts?

In planning and setting up your Internet site there are some areas where you will need either experts or expertise on your side.

HTML. If you have decided on a Web site as your Internet presence, you will need to design Web pages. HTML is the language that connects the graphics or text as they appear on the screen with Internet commands. For example, using HTML, you can designate a string of words as hypertext, so that clicking upon them will send the user to another page or even another site.

Do you have to learn HTML in order to establish a Web site? No. Not anymore. There are two ways to get around it:

1. Get an expert. The market is currently chock-full of HTML artists who will be eager to add HTML to your proposed site or even design your entire Web site for you. High competition has caused fees to sink from over $100 an hour just a couple of years ago to as low as $30 or even less today. HTML is easy to learn and almost anyone can declare themselves HTML artists. What counts, when selecting an HTML artist, is individual talent. If you decide to hire an HTML artist, be sure to ask for samples of his work before you sign a contract. Some high profile advertising agencies will charge you an arm and a leg to put together a Web site, but the end result may turn out to be worse than what a $30 an hour HTML artist would give you. The HTML artist must know who your potential customers are, or, for example, you might wind up owning a glitzy, ostentatious Web site that will alienate your content-minded customers.

2. Get a software. Not only are there plenty of Web page creator software about, but even some of today's desktop publishing software already include HTML design capabilities. They will allow you to create Web pages in minutes and submit them to your server service online. The price range for these software is usually $50-$200. No knowledge of HTML is required.

General consultation. Many questions are bound to pop up as you start the process of setting up your online business: which server service to use? What features should I include in my site? Should I add a Text-only option? You can of course hire a consultant to answer all these questions for you. Many consultants offer a complete "we'll-put-your-business-online" package. Choose carefully, however — their fees may be steep, and if your site is not too complex you may discover that you can find someone to answer your questions for free. Most likely, this someone is going to be your server service, who will no doubt take care of most technical matters for you.

Should you go along with every suggestion the server service's staff makes? Not necessarily. Make sure the features they are trying to sell you are actually beneficial for your business. There is usually a surcharge for each additional feature, and some server services may try to push them (for more detail, see page 43).

While planning your site, it is always a good idea to visit your competitors' sites. They might not always know what they are doing, but if they have been in business long enough they should at least know what *not* to do.

Conventional professional services. The services of lawyers and CPAs may prove essential for your business. Selling over the Internet sometimes involves exporting or licensing. For instance, if you sell alcohol online, you should be familiar with the procedure of verifying the customers' age before selling to them. You should know whether you should charge sales tax from your online customers, and the residents of which states to exclude from certain promotions. Flexible as an Internet business' address might be, it is still bound by the laws of the state or country it is located in.

Hiring experts would give you these advantages:

1. You will spend considerably less time working on the technical aspects of your business. This would mean leaving you more time to plan your business strategy and concentrate on the things you do best. Any economist will tell you that, "If he'll do your job and you'll do his job you'll both be out of a job."

2. There is a smaller chance of making mistakes that will hurt your business in the long run. Although you should never follow their advice blindly, experts have already been where you are going. They must know something.

3. Experts are likely to open your eyes to ideas and possibilities you never knew existed. They may change your whole approach to doing business online.

There are also advantages to doing everything yourself:

1. You save a lot of money.

2. You gain first hand experience. This experience will help you

with any future changes to your site, as you will not be dependant on experts to do it for you. You will be better equipped to adapt to new online technologies and features, and more aware of the online world and its components.

To sum it up, it is the old time-versus-money question. Which do you value more? If you can afford to hire experts and have more productive things to do with your time — hire them.

Budgeting

How much is setting up an online business going to cost you? It varies, of course, according to the size and type of business you wish to start and the professional services you choose to employ. Here is a short list that can give you some idea about the estimated expenses for an average online business:

❑ Connecting directly to the Internet (through a dedicated connection and your own UNIX workstation): $2,000-$50,000 plus $1,000-$2,000 a month.

❑ Establishing an Internet presence through a server service: $20-$500 plus $20-$300 a month.

❑ Setting up shop with an online mall: $0-$500 plus $5-$500 a month.

❑ Connecting through an independent (non-Internet) network: $10-$200 plus $10-$100 a month.

❑ BBS (setup): $1,500 and up.

❑ Web site designing (including HTML): $100-$10,000

❑ Other (conventional) business expenses (CPA, stationery, fees): $2,000 and up.

Total investment would range from next to nothing to several tens of thousands of dollars. The main factor in calculating the cost is manpower: to what degree will you have to rely on hired consultants and experts. Many small Internet businesses started out on a shoe string and their owners did almost everything themselves. Not all of them succeeded, of course, but the most they could have lost was the time they invested, which for many small entrepreneurs is not a prohibitive commodity.

Large investments do not guarantee success. An online business, however fully automated, is not government bonds. You will have to spend time and effort as well as money. Make a business plan. Maybe your projected income does not justify a large investment. Remember that only one or two percent of the visitors to your site are going to make a purchase and that you cannot expect to make any net income from your site for at least six months. A small, inexpensive Internet site that is designed to survive for years on a small budget is better than a huge, expensive site that would set you back tens of thousands of dollars and may produce the same initial results as a smaller site. Remember — you can always expand your site later or switch to a direct Internet connection if the number of visitors justifies this.

The bottom line is this: anyone can afford to start an Internet business. What you can't invest in capital you can more than make up for with an investment of time and effort. Whichever way you choose, you have to be realistic and understand that any business is a struggling business at first. It takes a long term commitment to succeed — not just starting capital.

Financing is not easy to get for an online business. The Internet is still new, unproven business grounds. The media sees it as the gold rush of the 20th century, but not so the banks. For them, this is still a speculative business, and they may be reluctant to share the risks with Internet entrepreneurs.

For this reason, you may not want to hand the loan officer your Internet business plan, ingenious and solid as it may be. If your proposed Internet business is an extension of a conventional business, apply for a loan for a conventional business purpose. For example, you can use the bank loan to pay for machinery for the conventional business, and use the money you intended to spend on that machinery to pay for your

Internet business. If you cannot get a business loan, apply for an all-purpose personal loan, or open up a line of credit with your bank. Your credit limit is probably going to be low in this case, definitely smaller than a business loan would be, but it may be all you need. If all else fails, and if you feel confident about your online business idea, you can always resort to your high interest rate credit cards.

Methods of Payment on the Internet

Paying for products and services on the Internet can be done in a number of ways, and your best bet is to allow your customers a choice between several payment methods to ensure that *everyone* will be able to do business with you.

A. **Doing it the conventional way**. Your customers send you checks; the checks clear; you send them the goods. Is this what the Internet was set up for? No. There are great disadvantages to this method:

1. It takes a long time. This defeats the purpose of the Internet.

2. It complicates international trade. Foreign customers will have to go to their local bank and have it issue a check drawn in U.S. dollars. In addition to the hassle, there is also a substantial fee for each of these checks. There is even worse to come — you cannot deposit such a foreign check directly to your account. Your bank will have to collect it first, and only then will the funds be made available to you. There is no clearance schedule for checks drawn on foreign banks, and the process will probably take a long time.

3. It is inconvenient. The customer will think twice before ordering something. Impulse-buys are thus reduced significantly.

B. **C.O.D.** payments. This method is even worse than the previous one. Many, if not most conventional (especially mail order) merchants do not allow their customers this option. Major faults:

1. It is expensive, requiring the customer to pay a C.O.D. surcharge for every delivery.

2. It involves a lot of paperwork and labor. You may find that even as a small business owner you would have to hire additional employees just to handle the extra processing work.

3. It complicates international trade.

C. Credit cards. A lot has been said about the supposed dangers of using credit cards over the Internet. It is nothing but a myth. Using credit cards over the telephone is no less risky. Credit card numbers can be and are stolen from conventional vendors' files and records, and this is probably easier to do than penetrating online businesses' computers in order to retrieve credit card information. However, for the online business community it does not matter if the public's fear of using credit cards over the Internet is justified or without basis. The fear is there and that is that. It is up to the online business community to assuage consumers' fears. Online businesses must offer consumers secure ways to process credit card orders even if they are redundant, because the future of Internet business transactions depends on it. There are different ways for merchants to process credit card orders and to secure them:

1. Encrypted credit card orders. The account information sent by the customer is encrypted, and cannot be decrypted without a code that is known only to the credit card processing company. There is virtually no way for unauthorized people to obtain the credit card information, and the customer feels safe; much safer than when submitting her credit card information over the telephone. Even if redundant, this feeling of security makes consumers feel comfortable shopping online.

   To be able to accept credit cards, you have to contact a processing company. The processing company will sell you a special software that enables customers to type in their credit card information, which you can then send directly to the company's processing center. Credit cards can be processed in real time, and, if authorized by the processing company, the customer's account will be debited and the amount (minus applicable processing charges) will be deposited directly to the merchant's bank account. This is not much different from the process that takes place when the customer is using his credit card to purchase items from a conventional retailer. One difference that exists between the two transactions is that an online merchant does not have to use the processing terminal and printer that a store owner must use.

Ask your credit card processing service (and your server service) to enable secure credit card transactions from your site.

There are many processing companies. For example:

ECS Global   http://www.e-transfer.com

Cardservice International
http://www.members.home.net/tasinet/merchant.html

Internet Commerce Solutions http://www.merchantaccounts.com

2. Taking credit card information over the phone. This is the simplest method. First, set up an account with a credit card processing company for processing phone orders. Your site will refer the customers who do not wish to use their cards online to a telephone number over which they can order your products. The obvious drawback of this option is the need to manually process the telephone credit card orders.

3. First Virtual (you can reach them at: http://www.fv.com) is a company that offers a service that combines the previous method with taking orders online. Their main advantage over the previous method is that they save you the time and trouble it takes to manually process telephone orders. What they do is simple: the customer phones them and leaves his credit card information with them. They give him a code (called VirtualPin). Whenever this customer needs to order an item from an online merchant who accepts First Virtual, he needs only to give that merchant his VirtualPin over the Internet. First Virtual will send that customer an e-mail message asking him to confirm the order he placed with the merchant within 24 hours. If the order is confirmed, the amount is deposited to the merchant's account.

Another advantage of this method is that just about any merchant can use it. Some merchants experience difficulties when they try to open an account with the regular credit card processing companies, who subject them to a thorough credit check. There are also disadvantages to this method — the settlement period (the time it takes funds to be deposited to your account) can be much longer than that of a regular processing company, and there are additional fees. First Virtual is no substitute for accepting credit cards directly, and you should try to open an account with a credit card processing company in any case, even if you do accept First Virtual codes or are using a similar service.

D. E-cash (electronic cash). This is a relatively new concept. It works this way:

The customer buys e-cash currency from a special bank. This electronic currency is downloaded into her account/computer. When that customer buys an item from an online vendor that accepts e-cash, the purchase sum is electronically deducted from her account. The electronic cash is then deposited to the merchant's special account, from which it can be drawn as (real) cash. Advantages:

1. Security. You don't use a credit card.

2. Privacy. No one will be able to look at your credit card statements and learn what you have bought recently or which services you have been using.

Disadvantages:

1. Inconvenience. You have to buy e-cash from a special vendor prior to being able to use it, and do so again whenever your e-cash credit runs out.

2. You actually have to pay before you buy, and no one will pay you interest for e-cash that is just lying there unused.

Currently, there is not much chance that too many of your customers will be using e-cash. Furthermore, as consumers' fear of using credit cards over the Internet is slowly assuaged, this relatively inconvenient method is likely to be less in demand in the future.

The two main issuers of online electronic currency are:

DigiCash (http://www.digicash.com)

Cyber Cash (http://www.cybercash.com)

To summarize — when planning the methods of payment your site is going to work with, be sure you allow customers a choice between at least these two options:

1. Instant, convenient payment.

2. Secure payment.

Chapter 5

PROMOTION AND ADVERTISING

No business can expect to gross dollar one if nobody knows about it, and this is particularly true for Internet businesses. Your site does not have a geographical location — no passers by are going to notice it as they would a newly opened store. An online site which is not linked, registered with search engines, or otherwise publicized simply does not exist!

There are two ways to promote an online business — paid advertising or promotion (free or otherwise). The Internet offers countless opportunities for free or paid promotion. You would definitely want to take advantage of at least the free promotional services found online. The only real question for you is whether or not to use paid advertising.

PROMOTION

Registering Your Business with Online Search Engines and Web Directories

This is probably the first thing you need to do once you have establish your site. You may have heard the names of some of the better known search engines: Yahoo (http://www.yahoo.com), Excite (http://www. excite.com), Lycos (http://lycos.com), Magellan (http://www. mckinley.com), InfoSeek (http://www.infoseek.com or, for Infoseek Ultra: http://ultra.infoseek.com/Home?pg=home.html), WebCrawler (http://webcrawler.com), Alta Vista (http:// www.altavista.digital.com). Many other, smaller search engines also exist on the Internet; some include as many sites as possible in their databases and others cater only to searchers with specific interests (such as business or education) in mind. Search engines allow their users to search their databases by keying in a word or a string of words. The search engine then presents the user with a list of all the Internet sites whose name or subject include that key word and their URLs (Internet addresses). The items on this list are hypertext — clicking on them will take the user to the selected site. The user may customize the search and ask the search engine to find only Web sites with the requested key word, or only Usenet newsgroups articles. Search engines are the most popular tool Internet users employ to find sites (either by name or description).

Registering your business with these search engines is easy — simply go to their Web sites, where you will click on an "Add a site" or "Add URL" hypertext, and the program will take it from there. In addition to your site's name you will probably want to submit a few keywords that will allow users to reach you by describing your business activities. For example, if you are opening an online tax preparation service, you would probably want to include the words: CPA, tax, consultant, business service, accountant, refund, 1040, etc. Make sure you add your site to the large search engines (see above), since they are usually Internet users' first choice and are made easily accessible to users by popular browsers such as Netscape or Microsoft Explorer.

Please note: Meta files (special, hidden files that can be attached to Web/HTML files) also allow you to enter your site's description and keywords. Make sure you use these files since they will allow even search engines you are not listed with to display this information to their users. Check your Web authoring software for instructions.

There are quicker, probably more efficient ways of registering your site with search engines and Web directories. Some online services will do it for you, offering a variety of services and fee structures that range from free to hundreds of dollars a month. Their advantage, of course, is that they save you time. It is a good idea to use at least the free options many of these services will give you. Make sure you supply them with the right key words and names — it will take you ages to change this information once your site is registered with the search engines. Here is a partial list of such online services:

❑ SUBMIT-IT (http://www.submit-it.com) allows you to register your service with up to 16 search engines for free or with many more if you pay a one time fee.

❑ THE SHOPPER (http://www.shoppingdirect.com/index.html). This is a directory that lets users view businesses by classification or by the products/services they offer. From their menu choose: "Submit your shopping site for our review" or "Send us a description of your site."

❑ ADD IT (http://www.liquidimaging.com/liqimg/submit) allows you to submit your site's URL to over 20 places on the Web for free.

❑ An excellent site for online entrepreneurs to visit is Oregon State University's *What's New Too*, which in addition to a What's New list also offers valuable information about online promotion, registration with search engines and Web directories, Virtual Libraries and more. To get there, first go to: http://nu2.com/ and from there click on the "Promoting your page" item.

❑ http://www.realitycom.com/bamboo/submit.html-ssi   (for description see page 74)

Links

Links can lead from your site to other sites or from other sites to yours. Either way, they will work for you. Customers will arrive at your site from other sites, and the displaying of links to other sites will enhance your site greatly — it will allow you to offer your customers more resources.

When choosing a site to link from, you should make sure that this site is relevant to your business and that it will send you the right kind of customers. It is not always enough that the linking site is a big company with thousands of visitors a day. For example, if your site deals with home owners insurance, there is not much point in establishing a link to it in an online travel agency's site. Customers arriving from there will probably be interested in travel insurance, which you do not sell.

How to place a link:

1. The simplest way is by e-mail. Contact the site you are interested in and ask them to establish a link to your site. Offer to reciprocate, but don't make it sound like a threat — "I've placed a link to *your* site — please link to mine or I will have to remove it," — this sounds horrible. If you intend to link your site to the site you are approaching, do so regardless of their willingness to reciprocate. If you are not interested in linking to a site, don't make promises. The approached site is probably going to check your site prior to establishing a link to it, so give them time to think it over.

2. Open one of the search engines and key in the word "link" or "links". You will be presented with the URLs of many sites that offer you at least one of the following services:

   A. A list of sites you can establish a link to your site from. These sites usually do this for free, but they might require you to place a reciprocal link to their site.

   B. Taking care of it for you. For a certain fee, these services will establish links to your site from a number of Web or other Internet sites.

A list of submit-services that would register your site with various directories and establish links to it from other sites can be found at:

http://www.realitycom.com/bamboo/submit.html-ssi

What's New

Since finding new sites is often all that matters to some Internet users, it is not surprising that Internet sites whose only business is to highlight new sites (especially Web sites) have mushroomed in recent years. Some of these sites are better known than others (such as Netscape's or Yahoo's *What's New* services) while others enjoy a more limited popularity. Getting your business' name into the big What's New lists is not easy; you have to shine brighter than thousands of your competitors, or pay a considerable sum for being mentioned. You stand a much better chance with the smaller What's New services. By their nature, any mention of your site by What's New services is temporary, but it should not be discounted. Internet users are starved for new things, and will search them out tirelessly. Some users who enter your site because it is new would never have considered visiting it otherwise. This mentality may seem a little weird, but as long as it is out there, you'll do best to indulge it. Some of the What's New services will allow you to enter your business name several times. Here are some of the more accessible (for a small business) What's New sites:

❑ Webcrawler's What's New:
http://webcrawler.com/select/nunu.new.html (Choose "Add your URL" to include your site).

❑ What's New on the Internet:
http://www.whatsnew.com/whatsnew/submit/   (submission page).

❑ What's New Too:
http://nu2.com/   This site promises to post your listing within 36 hours.

When sending your business description to What's New lists, keep in mind that the people who are viewing these lists are interested in knowing what is *new* about your online business. Save the usual, accurate description of your site (or your sales copy) for other kinds of listings and directories, and give the seekers of the new a reason to visit your site. For example, if you are selling sunglasses online, don't let the online community think of it as "Oh, another sunglass site — what's he doing in the What's New list, anyway?" You have to give them something new and special, such as a unique feature that shows visitors how the different sunglass types you have look on a model (by displaying different pictures of this model when different types of sunglasses are clicked on). Maybe you want to play down the commercial aspect of the site and dedicate only 20-30% of it to the actual selling, while saving the rest for displaying comprehensive, large information resources and links. Give this information a special edge: "sun damage to the unprotected eye" for example. With this, you now have a description in the What's New listing that offers both freshness and free access to interesting information. Now they *are* going to visit your site — both potential customers and curious maybes.

Press Releases

Don't forget conventional promotion. This important rule refers mostly to press releases. An online business is first and foremost a business, and a business should be promoted in any effective way, online *and* off-line. People who are connected to the Internet, let's not forget, also watch television, listen to the radio and read newspapers. This is the reason for the abundance of Internet addresses (usually Web sites' URLs) found today in newspaper/magazine ads and TV commercials.

Press releases are a common way of promotion for every type of business. Manufacturers use them to introduce new products about to be released to the market, writers to promote a book, telecommunication companies to present new features. If you have a new Web site, then you, too, have a new product to tell people about. Today, new Web sites often receive the same attention that new books and products do. A Web site, therefore, is not just a business presence — it has become a product in its own right.

There are two kinds of newspapers whose editors may be interested in an Internet site's press release:

1. Internet newspapers (online and paper based), who, as their subject matter suggests, take great interest in the online world and related developments. Don't forget, however, that thousands of new Internet sites are being opened every day, and that many of them may be similar to yours. "Just another online sunglass shop" will not receive much attention by these magazines; not unless it features a new gimmick or a new online business concept that might interest readers. Bottom line — to get a

magazine who deals with the online world interested, you have to concentrate on the Internet aspects of your business (technical or innovative) rather than on the business itself.

Two of these magazines are:

❑ *Internet World*
20 Ketchum St'
Westport CT 06880
Telephone: 1-800-573-3062

❑ *Wired*
544 2nd St'
San Francisco, CA 94107
Telephone: 1-800-769-4733

Also check the following newsgroup: alt.journalism

2. Newspapers dealing with specific subjects or businesses. For instance, if your site sells (and displays information about) aircraft communication equipment, it might interest a magazine like Plane & Pilot. Although not an Internet magazine, Plane & Pilot may view your business as an aircraft industry related business with an innovative twist. Many magazines and newspapers today feel that ignoring the Internet means staying behind, and they are on the lookout for any excuse to write about the online world. Being mentioned in specializing magazines has another advantage for you: you reach your target audience. In the above example, there is no doubt that you will find more customers for aircraft communication systems in Plane & Pilot than in any of the Internet magazines.

How do you write a press release? First, go to the library and prepare a list of all the magazines that your potential customers might be reading. You can even send press releases to foreign magazines — their readers can find you just as easily as would a reader of the neighborhood paper. In addition to paper based newspapers/magazines, you should also consider online magazines (zines). You can find links to thousands of newspapers with a Web presence at: http://www.ecola.com/news

Rules for writing a press release:

1. The press release should be about one page long, unless the magazine you submit it to encourages longer pieces (and publishes them in full).

2. Don't make it too self serving. Remember — the editor's goal is not to promote your business, but to make the article interesting for the magazine's readers. Make it interesting, and you will have greatly increased your press release's chances of being published.

3. Unless you are a well known expert in your field, leave your own biography out of it. The names of executives or employees should be mentioned only if they are quoted.

4. Tell the readers what you can do for them, but with no sales pitch. Make it look as if the magazine itself has written it. Often, the editors will leave your press release as is. If you make them alter or cut it because of either sales copy or bad grammar you may find that the message you originally wanted to convey to potential customers is no longer there.

5. Your site must have a unique edge, the hook that will make visiting it a must for everyone who reads your press release.

6. Tell the editor what is the earliest release date for your press release. If the site is already established (and functioning) write: "For immediate release" on top of your document.

7. A kill date is the last date you allow the release to be published on. Writing "No kill date" at the top of the release means there is no such limit.

8. End your release with either -30- or * * * .

9. The release copy must be double spaced, so as to make it easier for editors to add their corrections/changes to it.

Here is an example of a press release:

For immediate release. No kill date.

Contact: George Davis

Kansas City, November 17th 1996 — ABCD Database (http://www.....), a Kansas city based consulting firm, will allow Internet users access to a new online service — stolen vehicle alert.

Is the car or motorcycle you are about to buy stolen? With title forgeries and sophisticated car-thief rings, this may be hard to tell. For a search fee of $4.00, **ABCD Database** will perform a thorough search using the V.I.N you give them, and will tell you within seconds whether or not the car or bike you are about to purchase is included in the hot list of stolen vehicles.

In addition to the above service, the site offers a useful guide for used car buyers, numerous articles concerning car alarms and locking devices, and even some hints on reducing your fire/theft insurance premiums. If you still have questions that the articles found in the site did not answer, ABCD's consultants will try to answer them through e-mail as soon as possible.

Another feature of the site is, of course, links. "We are connected to at least thirty similar sites, all of which offer good advice on anti-theft and other security devices and methods," says ABCD's Webmaster, Steve Brown.

-30-

Sending press releases through e-mail is a quick, inexpensive way of reaching hundreds of magazine editors, but this is no substitute for sending hard copies through land mail (at least to important contacts). There are a few simple rules to follow if you choose to e-mail your release:

> ➤ The first part of your e-mail message must be a short, succinct description of your business and of the attached press release. Newspaper editors receive hundreds of press releases, and many of these are completely irrelevant to the subject matter of the newspaper or are simply not interesting enough for the editor. Some editors may be reluctant to read through a long, unsolicited press release, and will appreciate your consideration in giving them the gist of it first.

> ➤ Send the release to the editors' work e-mail address, not to their home e-mail address.

> ➤ Although it is tempting to leave the job of distributing your press releases to a public relation service, keep in mind that editors will most likely know that the press release was prepared by such a service, and may resent it. Sending these e-mail messages one at a time and making sure they do not read like form letters will help to make a much better impression on the editor.

> ➤ Do not call editors to check on the status of your press release. They receive hundreds of unsolicited press releases in the course of a month. Don't expect a reply to your e-mail (or land mail) message either, for the same reason. However, if you are sending your press release through land mail, enclosing a self addressed envelope or a return slip will greatly improve your chances of getting a response.

Press releases must be sent on an ongoing basis, sometimes as often as once a month, in order to produce results. Many press releases were published only after their 10th or 15th copy has reached the editor (usually this would be the same editor who had ignored this release before).

Radio/TV Interviews

Radio and TV interviews can and should be used to promote your site. How to arrange for them? The key, again, is the interest and curiosity your site manages to arouse in the media people. It is extremely hard, as you might expect, to get on Oprah or any of the big networks' talk shows and news reports; but there are also several thousands of local television and radio stations that are craving for something new to report on or interesting people to interview. Present them with a new concept they have never heard before (or that they hope to cover in their shows) that will allow them to do their journalistic duty and present their viewers or listeners with something of interest, and they will give you exposure. The features that the media finds interesting may be only secondary technical aspects of your site, but as long as it gives you exposure — who cares?

If an interview by a remote local TV station requires you to spend a long time in travel, you may want to reconsider. Will a small station give you enough exposure to justify the trip? The Internet is an international medium, and although local promotion should not be discounted, paying too much for it, even in terms of time and effort, may not be worth your while. The best solution is probably radio stations. You can be interviewed by telephone and spend literally minutes on each such interview — you don't even have to try on new clothes or put on makeup.

You have to send talk shows and business/news programs a letter (a.k.a. *media flier*) describing your site and any interesting subjects you would like to talk about. If they are interested they will contact you. Visit a library for listings of radio and TV stations.

Radio and TV stations are not supposed to charge you for interviews. Those who do, have very small audiences, so you should not bother with them in the first place.

On-Site Promotion

On site promotion may not make Internet users aware of the existence of your site, but it can ensure a better word-of-mouth advertising, and make your site appear more inviting and appealing in your ads or press releases. Here are a few on-site promotions you can try in your site:

1. Sweepstakes. This proven tactic rarely harms a business. As a merchant, the best prize you can offer is your own products or services. You can allow your visitors to participate anonymously, but the best online business approach is to make them enter their personal information (especially e-mail address). By doing this, you will have gained three advantages:

    A. The visitor interacts with your business rather than remain a mute observer.

    B. You can compile a list of potential customers' e-mail addresses.

    C. You will gather demographic information that will help you (and advertisers) to better understand who your customers are.

2. Quizzes. These are similar to sweepstakes, with the exception that the customer has to show a certain degree of knowledge of your area of business or line of products in order to qualify for a prize. The customer, therefore, is made to take an interest in your business. You don't want to make the questions too hard, or visitors to your site will be turned off. The quiz should also be of a general nature. For example, a film manufacturer's Internet site can present its visitors with questions about black and white photography techniques. People like to put their knowledge of general subjects or trivia to the test, but have little motivation to show any knowledge of a particular company.

3. Contests. Unlike a quiz, participants in a contest have to do something better than everyone else. Everyone may answer a quiz correctly, but with a contest there is only one winner, one prize to give away (and maybe some smaller, second or third prizes). The contest, of course, has got to be related to your business. The film manufacturer in the above example can hold a best-landscape-photograph contest, and offer a lifetime supply of film as first prize.

4. A constantly changing feature. For example, the film manufacturer can display a Photo-of-the-Day in its Web site. Amateur
photographers might drop in from time to time just to see this
changing exhibition. Another feature could be free (related)
software that visitors to your site could download (freeware).

5. Links. The film manufacturer's site can make itself "The first
place on the Internet an amateur photographer would want to
visit" by linking to all similar and related sites. In other words,
you can turn your site into a small Web directory.

All the above features are designed to keep visitors coming back to your
site and make them want to send their friends there. Such promotion will
probably help your business, but keep in mind that it requires constant
maintenance and updating, and may greatly increase the time you have
to spend working on your site. If you are a one person operation who on
top of everything else still keeps a day job, this type of promotion may
not be for you.

Online Malls

Even if you have established your online presence through a server
service, online malls (see page 43) can be good promotional tools. *The
Internet Mall,* for instance, the best known, probably oldest online mall,
offers a basic listing for $48 a year. It is open for any online shop that
has a tangible product or service for sale, and that allows customers to
order them through the Internet. This mall (a.k.a. Dave Taylor's Internet
Mall) can be found at: http://www.internet-mall.com. Choose the
"Adding your shop" hypertext. The Internet Mall claims to be the world's
largest shopping site. It currently lists over 25,000 merchants. The mall
also offers a premier listing that, for $360 a year, allows merchants more
space on the site and the use of advanced features.

There are, of course, hundreds of other online malls out there. For a
directory of 500 of them, go to:

http://nsns.com/MouseTracks/HallofMalls.html

Newsgroups

Sounds easy, doesn't it? If you are in the business of, say, selling dog food, all you have to do is find a newsgroup dedicated to pets and post your commercial messages there. Well — don't even think about it!

Newsgroups users are probably the most anti-commercial group of the Internet community. Contaminating their newsgroup with commercial messages (spamming) is considered by many users the worst online vice imaginable. It is not likely that such an ad will bring the business that posts it too many customers. Instead, it may bring about the following results:

1. The newsgroup community may flame you, that is — flood your e-mail address with hundreds of hate messages.

2. Even worse, some of the more belligerent newsgroup users may take it upon themselves to embark on a defamation crusade against you. They might post (to the same newsgroup) dozens of false complaints and accusations against you and your business that will cause you a lot of harm.

3. Alienating the users of a newsgroup that deals with the subject of your own business means alienating potential customers. Even people who may have needed to use your business services would search high and low for your competitors, who did not post unsolicited commercial messages to their favorite newsgroups.

So, how can you make newsgroups work for you? With caution and tact, and with an attitude of an insider who wants to contribute to the group rather than a vendor who's in it for the money. Avoid transparent attempts to deceive the newsgroup users by posting messages like "I've heard of a good place to buy Rock & Roll CDs online. Their address is: http://....." Anyone who had spent more than ten minutes browsing through newsgroup postings would recognize the true nature of such a message right away.

For a newsgroup posting to work, it has to be solicited. For example, if someone asks "My Dog has fleas. What should I do?" this is your chance to answer him. This answer, however, must be free of all commercial hype. It should address this specific question and no more. "ABCD Enterprises sells flea powder. Their URL is....." is a short, concise reply that does not smell of a commercial ad and will not be resented by anyone. You may ruin it for yourself if your reply turns out to be a plug and includes self praise and a detailed description of the range of products your business sells. As you probably realize by now, promoting your business through newsgroups requires constant monitoring of newsgroup postings and waiting for the right opportunities. It will also help if your site offers free service or information. As long as they know they do not have to pay for it, newsgroup readers will not mind checking your site out. Don't try to deceive them, however, or this tactic will backfire. If you promote your site as a free Web site, any commercial service or product must be downplayed and offered only as an option. Postings to newsgroups are rolled off the board after a few days, so you have to check them at least twice a week.

Finding the newsgroups you need among the thousands of newsgroups that exist (and their number is continually growing) can be time consuming. Fortunately, there is help. Sites such as DejaNews (http://www.dejanews.com) are dedicated to searching newsgroups by subject matter. For example, if you are selling custom car seat covers online, and are looking for the right newsgroups to monitor, keying in the word "auto" will display all the newsgroups that deal with cars or the auto industry, such as: rec.autos.driving; misc.transport.urban-transit; rec.autos.marketplace.

You can also create your own newsgroup, but be aware that while doing so is relatively easy, keeping it alive is not. No one will participate in a self serving newsgroup except to tell the other participants what he thinks of it. Maintaining a newsgroup takes a commitment and requires a non-commercial attitude.

Direct E-mail

In a word — don't! Unlike conventional junk mail, which may be disposed of without opening the envelope, direct e-mail messages take time to download and read. Unsolicited direct e-mail is a sure way to alienate the entire Internet population, and to ensure that no one will want to do business with you.

The only way to harness direct e-mail to your promotional effort is if the customer specifically requests to be put on your mailing list. For example, your Internet site may include the option: "Please let me know by e-mail of new products and developments in the motorcycle industry." A customer who has visited your site and selected this option will welcome your e-mail messages and, being occasionally reminded of the existence of your site, may even come back to visit it again. See also *Mailing lists*, page 50.

PAID ADVERTISING

There are two forms of paid advertising: commercial ads and direct marketing.

Placing Ads

1. Placing ads in Internet sites. Many online businesses earn their living by accepting commercial advertising. The price is set according to the number of hits the site that accepts advertising records (see page 16). Some of the more popular search engines charge over $1,000 a week for a small ad+link, while the less popular sites may set you back only a couple of hundred a year. It is, of course, better to place your ad in sites that your potential customers are likely to visit. Advertising in such sites would cost less per potential customer than advertising in the large, popular sites. Before placing an ad with any of the Web sites, make sure you check their traffic records, which they can obtain from measuring services (see pages 16, 299).

2. Placing ads in conventional media — TV, radio and the press. Conventional means of advertising should not be neglected. However, the Internet has an international appeal, while local media does not. You have to ask yourself how many TV viewers, radio listeners or magazine readers have Internet access, and remember that only a small percentage of *those* will respond to

your ad. Will this be enough to cover the cost of the ad?

Paid advertising of any kind should be planned meticulously. Unsuccessful campaigns have been known to bring down many businesses. When placing an ad, you should ask yourself not only how many people are going to see your ad, but also the following:

➤ How many of the people who will see the ad are really your customers? For example, let us assume that you are selling hearing aids online. You have decided to publish an ad in a newspaper that is read by senior citizens. Only 5% of this newspaper's readers have Internet access. The result? You wind up spending 95% of your advertising budget on people who will never be able to visit your site, who may even feel alienated by your ad because of this. Another example: you have decided to advertise the same product in a popular Web site. Anyone who sees your ad has access to the Internet, of course, but how many of these visitors are senior citizens? So, where are you going to place such an ad? The answer is probably — either in Internet sites that senior citizens are likely to visit (e.g., sites that deal with health issues), or not at all. Anything else is going to be a waste of money.

➤ Is the market large enough to cover the cost of your ads? Sometimes ads succeed as planned, but the merchant still goes out of business. If, for example, you are selling a special kind of fly swatter, you may find that people, even if they prefer your brand to all other brands, do not buy enough fly swatters in the course of a year to justify a costly advertising campaign.

➤ Do you have anything to say? "Online Hardware Store" will not motivate people to jot down your Internet address and visit you the first chance they get. If all you sell is the usual product at the usual price, save your advertising money — no one will care. In other words, if you intend to use paid advertising to promote your online business, plan this business — especially tempting prices and special or unusual features — accordingly. Make sure you have bait before you go fishing.

➤ Can you afford to keep placing your ad for at least six months without counting on it for income? One or two ads will never work (unless you are selling quarters for fifteen cents apiece). Only a continued presence over a long time will persuade your potential customers of your business' seriousness; only then will you see the orders starting to pour in from your ad.

Direct Land Mail (not e-mail!)

This can be an efficient, economical.form of paid advertising, but only if you start out with a good mailing list. Defining a good mailing list is very easy: it is a list of people who are most likely to use your services. *Finding* a good mailing list is much harder. Some companies, especially magazines and list brokers, sell or rent them (when rented you can use them only once), but you have to make sure the mailing list you buy or rent consists of people who:

1. Have Internet access.

2. Are known to have bought a product or service similar to the ones you are selling, and *recently*.

Direct mailings can be cost effective if you share-an-envelope with several other businesses. These businesses must not be competitors, of course, but all the merchants in the same direct mailing package must have an online presence. The Internet is still a new, interesting concept, and people who have Internet access will probably not be able to resist opening an envelope marked "Products and services you can buy on the Internet." Search the library for directories such as *Direct Marketing List Source* for lists of thousands of mailing lists and brokers.

Summary

How to Make Your Internet Site Work:

1. Give your customers an incentive to visit your site. This incentive can be a low price, hard to get items, interesting information, gimmicks, sweepstakes, and a variety of other features.

2. Take advantage of all the free promotion opportunities you can find.

3. Don't forget conventional promotion — the media can also be utilized to promote your online business.

4. Update and make changes to your site at least once a month in order to help create repeat customers.

5. In a Web site, offer a text-only option in order to widen your customer base.

6. Use plain, small graphics to make your Web site "fast".

7. Generate your income in several ways to keep your site going — sell products, services, information, advertising, work with drop shippers. Don't put all your eggs in one basket.

8. If you choose to set up your online business as a Web site, you may want to run a parallel auto responder or Gopher site. Users' response will soon tell you whether you should continue with these features or stick to a strictly Web site business.

9. Make it easy for customers to buy from your site. Allow them several payment options: credit cards, secure transactions, checks, e-cash.

10. Above all, and regardless of the type of business you plan or promotion you choose — know how to wait! There is little chance of your business becoming an overwhelming success

during its first months, and even year, of operation; few businesses show net income during their first year. It may sound corny, but succeeding in business does take perseverance, time and struggle.

And A Final Word,

Have no doubt about it — you will make mistakes; everyone does. The question is: how much will these mistakes cost you? Online promotion costs little; paid advertising costs a lot. If your business is small or medium (and this includes businesses that gross $1,000,000 a year), your advertising budget should be equally small. Start out with free online and conventional promotion, and *only* if you get good results, make a tentative attempt at paid advertising. Save your money — your business is going to need it to survive that first hard year that is ahead.

> For additional information, don't forget to visit Actium Publishing's own Web site at: http://www.actium1.com/home

SECTION II

121 INTERNET BUSINESSES YOU CAN START FROM HOME

Note:

Each of the 121 online businesses in this section may cover more than just one business idea. For example, *Home Made Food Items* is a title that covers hundreds of potential businesses that sell: sauces, beverages, pastries, spices, dried fruit, etcetera. Even starting a bee hive in your backyard and selling honey through the Internet falls withing this category. For this reason, you don't have to follow any of these 121 business ideas to the letter. They are supposed to educate, open your eyes to new possibilities, and help you find your own niche, your own unique path.

The businesses whose online addresses are given under "Find a similar business at" are not necessarily the finest examples of their particular category, neither are the products or services they offer promoted in this book in any way. They are mentioned here merely as sites that deal with the types of businesses discussed in this book.

When keying in URLs, please note the difference between (-) and (_), as well as between *html* and *htm*. Also, URLs are case sensitive, so use uppercase and lowercase letters as written in this book.

1. AUTO LOAN BROKER

This type of business has been around for as long as cars are sold. People's need for a car far outweighs most other financial considerations, and they are often willing to spend more on it than they have — in other words, they take out a loan. The number of potential customers for this business is almost unlimited. Not only does the number of car owners grow steadily, but even people who already own cars replace them (especially if these are old models) every couple of years.

The first thing you have to do is pick a few lenders to work with. Contact them and inquire about their approval policy — there is little point in working with lenders who are as tough as banks are, because most of your customers are probably going to come to you after they have been rejected by banks. Naturally, you will also have to come to an agreement with the lender about commissions and fees.

Next, you have to advertise. This is where the Internet comes in. As a broker who acts only as a middleman between the lender and the customer, you have no geographical limitations. Unlike conventional brokers, who are usually limited to advertisements in local auto-market magazines, you can reach customers all over the U.S.

Start-up investment (other than Internet site costs and connection fees): $1,000-$5,000

International potential: None — unless you persuade lenders to work with people who cannot be checked through the usual credit reporting agencies.

Special promotional strategies (in addition to those discussed in chapter 5): Link to and from as many automobile related sites as you can, as well as online lenders (even mortgage brokers). Send your press releases to local used car market papers. Offer tips for used car buyers in your site, as well as advice on finding low premium insurance companies and other related services.

Qualifications needed: None.

Educating yourself: Learn all you can about lenders and financial institutions. Read every book you can find about these subjects, and make phone inquiries (banks, lenders, CPA's).

Number of employees needed to start business (apart from yourself): 0

Things to watch out for: Wasting too much time on people who have no chance of getting approved. This line of business requires a high degree of persistence. Not every lender will want to work with you.

Additional income: You can sell information (through e-mail, for instance) and short guides about applying for car loans, finding a reliable car dealer, etc. You can sell advertising space to car dealers and financial institutions.

Find a similar business at: http://www.nfgroup.com

2. BANKRUPTCY CONSULTANT

Unfortunately, bankruptcies and bankruptcy consultants are here to stay. No one wants to imagine himself landing in bankruptcy, and yet many thousands become insolvent every year. For some, it is something they prepared, even planned, for years ahead. For most, it is a shocking, degrading experience, a horrible blow that shatters them. These are victims — people who lost financial control due to faulty financial planning, unforeseen hardships, or temptation.

These people, whose world came crushing down on them, usually know nothing about their rights and the possibilities that are open before them. For some, this is the end of the world. They may find themselves having to spend thousands of dollars they do not have on lawyers and court fees they may not need. The consultant's job is to assess their financial situation, and to break down their overwhelming sense of despair into a detailed, reassuring plan that will get them back on their feet as soon as possible.

The Internet allows you to reach a wide audience, but it also eliminates the personal touch that some of the more difficult cases may require. Therefore, you are limited to just two online bankruptcy services:

1. Selling packages of information. A few months before they actually go bankrupt, many people will try to find out as much as they can about the process. Although not in need of immediate help, they may want to know their rights and possibilities — perhaps to assess whether going into bankruptcy is a good solution for them, or whether they should try to pay their heavy debts after all.

2. Online one-on-one consulting. This can be done either by e-mail or by talking to customers through chat programs (either vocal or text-based). In most cases, such consultations will be enough and no personal meeting will have to be arranged.

Start-up investment (other than Internet site costs and connection fees): $1,000-$5,000

International potential: None.

Special promotional strategies (in addition to those discussed in chapter 5): Link to and from sites that offer financial consultation. Watch for related questions in newsgroups. As this is a painful subject, convincing newspaper editors that you are there to help people in need rather than to make a buck on their misfortune will get your press releases published in many newspapers. For this reason alone it is worth your while to offer tremendous amounts of free information on your site, as well as FAQ files and links.

Qualifications needed: None (unless you want to represent your customers in court).

Educating yourself: Books, courses, seminars. Be prepared to consult other consultants or even lawyers for your first few cases, even if it means losing money on them.

Number of employees needed to start business (apart from yourself): 0

Things to watch out for: Some of your customers (especially those referred to you by newspaper articles or word of mouth), may not have Internet access. Be prepared to offer your consultation service over the phone and to send a hard copy of your information through land mail if necessary.

In this business, you need to be tactful — you are dealing with people who are going through what is probably the hardest period of their lives.

Additional income: Other financial services. Using your reputation to arrange seminars.

Find a similar business at: http://www.kci-usa.com

3. ONLINE WAREHOUSE/PRICE CLUB

Warehouses or price clubs buy bulk odd lots and make them available to the public at dirt-cheap prices provided the customer buys a certain quantity of the item. This way, customers buy a year's supply of an item, but pay below wholesale. The problem is, many customers make the trip to the warehouse only to discover that it stocks nothing of interest for them that week.

By offering the same service online, you can save customers the trip and the uncertainty. Searching through your menu, they can find out immediately what is available that day and at what price. This also ensures that they will visit your site frequently to see if any new products were added. You can keep your site simple and text-only (even on the

Web) because your low prices are your hook.

There are two different approaches to this business:

1. Buying and stocking all the items you are offering your customers.

2. Becoming a middleman. You display other (conventional) warehouse's items, or items that you will purchase only after they have been ordered. This is not unlike drop shipping.

Another service you can perform in your site is to allow customers to display their own bulk lots or other under-wholesale priced items on your site (for a commission).

Start-up investment (other than Internet site costs and connection fees): Not including inventory: $1,000-$5,000.

International potential: Yes. In fact, as such opportunities are rarer in most other countries, this site can be very popular there, and especially if the items on your site are expensive enough to justify the costs of international shipment.

Special promotional strategies (in addition to those discussed in chapter 5): This business is of a general appeal, and should be linked to and from any site that shows substantial traffic. The same applies to newspapers and other channels of advertising. Whenever you manage to offer a good deal on a certain item, however, you should try to promote it in the appropriate sites or newsgroups. Set up a mailing list, as many people will probably want to be added to it and receive notifications of new deals and items through their e-mail boxes. The best thing about this business is that once you've got a customer, you are probably going to keep him.

Qualifications needed: None.

Educating yourself: Study the market. Search newspapers for ads concerning business opportunities, merchandise for sale and auctions.

Number of employees needed to start business (apart from yourself): 1-3. This business may involve a lot of search and going to different auctions or job lots. It may also require you to put someone in charge of processing sales and another employee in charge of contacting various warehouses.

Things to watch out for: This business involves constant updating of your site. For large or heavy items, shipping and handling costs can take the edge off your low prices.

Additional income: An online classified ad (merchandise for sale) section on your site.

Find a similar business at:
http://www.grandmart.com.hk/

4. CANDLE MANUFACTURER

This is one of the easiest and least expensive businesses to start online. Candles can be made in a variety of ways, from molding to sculpting, and their mark-up is huge. You can either buy ready-made candle molds, make your own, or find an original way for turning your own unique designs into candles. Sell religious candles, scented, household, decorative, hand painted, etcetera. Your site will naturally have to include a lot of graphics, and allow your customers to view your unique craftsmanship and to choose the items they like. For that reason, you would probably want to get a good camera (or better yet, a professional photographer) and an inexpensive ($100-$200) scanner. The quality of the photos you display on your site must be at least as good as the quality of the candles themselves.

Start-up investment (other than Internet site costs and connection fees): $1,000-$2,000

International potential: Yes.

Special promotional strategies (in addition to those discussed in chapter 5): Link to and from any sites that deal with crafts, art, gifts, or religion. Send press releases to magazines that deal with these subjects. Do not consider paid advertising as the market is probably too small to realize a profit from it.

Qualifications needed: None.

Educating yourself: One or two books about candle making and crafts, a bit of practice — and you're there.

Number of employees needed to start business (apart from yourself): 0

Things to watch out for: Competition. What you need most are original designs and good craftsmanship.

Additional income: Expanding into other crafts: decorations, miniatures, handweaving, pottery. Selling candlesticks.

Find a similar business at:
http://www.frii.com/~candles/index.html

5. PARENTING CENTER (YOUNG CHILDREN)

Children are here to stay. So are parents' spending on them. Setting up an Internet site that deals with a variety of subjects that parents find interesting will be tapping into a tremendous market potential.
The site can offer information on available child care services

(nationwide), new baby products and toys, new medical services, and also comprehensive referral lists (plus links or addresses) of: children party organizers, clowns, new children's book reviews, new educational games and video cassettes, children's furniture, reviews of plays and entertainment events aimed at young children, tutors, security devices for tots, baby products, special food items, vitamins.

Set up a mailing list, and allow free exchange of information between parents. A FAQ composed of parents' questions should be displayed in the site. A free notice board that allows parents to exchange old baby clothes or other items can also be set in the site. Another attraction could be a collection of bedtime stories parents could print out (or, if you put them on audio files, play for the children). You can add a feature that will encourage young children to send (with the help of their parents) letters to their relatives or friends in other states through your site. The letters will be written using a special form that will enable children to choose colorful fonts and graphics, and they will be converted into land mail or FTP files.

You can derive your income from:

1. Accepting advertising. With the potential of attracting many visitors, this site may become an ideal spot for baby products manufacturers to place their ads on.

2. Selling products: children's books, vitamins, toys.

3. Selling services (see the letter writing service above).

4. Consultation services (especially for young couples).

5. Selling complete information packages. For example, a complete party planner: games, what and where to buy, where to get professional entertainment, how to make decorations, etcetera.

You should not charge a subscription fee to enter your site (this is the wrong business approach to almost any Internet site).

Start-up investment (other than Internet site costs and connection

fees): $1,000 — $50,000

International potential: Yes.

Special promotional strategies (in addition to those discussed in chapter 5): Link to and from sites that deal with family issues. Keep an eye on related newsgroups. Send press releases to child care, health and fitness, and women's magazines.

Qualifications needed: None.

Educating yourself: Consultation, experience, books.

Number of employees needed to start business (apart from yourself): 0

Things to watch out for: For this site to work, it must be very large. It will probably require a mailing list of its own and one or two mailbots in addition to the main Web site. You will have to spend a lot of time collecting and updating the vast, diversified information you have to display on your site in order to make it work. The commercial nature of the business must be downplayed or it will never become the Mecca for parents it is supposed to be. Although the site must be huge, take care not to overwhelm the visitor. Present clear, simple menus or directories at your home page.

Additional income: An online family center.

Find a similar business at:
http://www.tnpc.com/

6. COLLEGE APPLICATION SERVICE

With the huge number of colleges and courses out there, many high school graduates feel confused and overwhelmed when they are faced with the decision of choosing their future site of learning. The amount of data available on the subject is stupendous, and gathering it entails spending hundreds of hours doing research, browsing through various publications, and making numerous phone calls.

A site that offers its visitors an easy, organized access to this information is exactly what high school students and parents need and what high school advisors do not always provide. Your main sources of income will be online consultation and the selling of packages of specific information on certain colleges and applications. Rating colleges is also a very important service, and especially if the college in question is located in a remote city or state and is therefore unknown to the applicant.

You might want to set a special feature in your site that will guide applicants who have not been admitted to the college of their choice, and advise them on special programs, courses or text books that can help them improve their chances in the future.

Start-up investment (other than Internet site costs and connection fees): $1,000-$5,000

International potential: Yes (advising foreign applicants who wish to study in the united States).

Special promotional strategies (in addition to those discussed in chapter 5): Establishing links in any site that appeals to teenagers or their parents is a good idea. Offer as many links as possible in your site that will allow your customers to visit the institutions they are interested in (if those institutions have an online presence), as well as a variety of databases. If your site offers free information, it will be possible to contact school newspapers and ask their editors to mention your site. Ask visitors to participate by posting their comments on their colleges, and by sharing their experience with new applicants. A mailing list may also be a good idea for this site.

Qualifications needed: None.

Educating yourself: You must dedicate at least several weeks to research. Call every college you intend to include in your site and ask for information packages. Search the libraries for publications that deal with the subject and rate educational institution.

Number of employees needed to start business (apart from yourself): 0

Things to watch out for: The problems of some of your customers may be thornier than you expect. Be prepared to invest the time and trouble it takes to solve these problems, as well as the money that long distance calls to remote colleges may cost you. Try to limit all contacts to e-mail messages.

Additional income: Accepting advertising. Also, you can expand into college loan consulting or brokering, since financing is one of the most serious problems many applicants have to face. You can even adopt a whole different approach to this business by offering, free of charge, all the services described above and basing your income solely on financial aid consulting.

Find a similar business at:
http://www.collegexpress.com/index.html

7. ONLINE GENEALOGIST

This business seems to have been created especially for the Internet. It involves nothing but the exchange of information between the business operator and the consumer. The initial investment here is minimal, but operating this kind of business requires extensive research. For some of the harder searches, in particular when searching archives located in a foreign country, you may need to work with local genealogists and adjust your fees accordingly.

Your site can include free services such as a database of as many family names as possible. Contact with clients can easily be made through e-mail. You can also sell related books and guides for amateur genealogists.

Start-up investment (other than Internet site costs and connection fees): $1,000-$5,000

International potential: Yes.

Special promotional strategies (in addition to those discussed in chapter 5): Try to establish links to and from sites that deal with family and ethnic issues. Send press releases to general interests, history, and regional magazines.

Qualifications needed: None.

Educating yourself: You may want to purchase several data resources (arranged by family name or geographical location) in the form of lists compiled by genealogists, census bureau reports and local archives. Search the Internet for online genealogical resources (there are plenty).

Number of employees needed to start business (apart from yourself): 0

Things to watch out for: Accepting hard cases that are beyond your abilities will cause you to waste a lot of time for a relatively small fee.

Additional income: Family trees. Compiling and selling lists (e.g., regional).

Find a similar business at: http://www.gentree.com

8. ONLINE HANDWRITING ANALYST

This type of business has one major limitation: if your customers want a quick analysis of their handwriting, they must have scanners in order to send you samples. If they do not have them, they will have to mail or fax these samples over to you. However, you will still be able to send them your analysis through e-mail.

Although hand writing analysis can easily be done through mail, graphologists have always been limited to their local communities. They could not afford nationwide advertising. Not anymore. The Internet will bring the word about your business to a wide, even international audience.

Large corporations and many institutions use graphologists to help them assess the personality of an individual or determine whether a certain document is a forgery or whether it is the genuine article. Point your online visitors to these services. Encourage small business owners to send in samples of job applicants' handwritings for analysis. Allow larger corporations (who do not want to keep a graphologist on the payroll) to open an account with your business and pay you on a monthly basis. An inexpensive ($200 - $400) scanner is a very small investment for such companies, and most of them already own one. An executive in one of these companies would only have to request a handwriting sample from an applicant, scan it, send you the sample and receive a reply within the day or even the hour. It is a service many of them will wonder how they ever managed without.

Start-up investment (other than Internet site costs and connection fees): $1,000-$10,000

International potential: Yes.

Special promotional strategies (in addition to those discussed in chapter 5): Go after corporate accounts. Send them direct land mail (not unsolicited e-mail!) describing your services. Establish links in sites that offer services for businesses. Allow individual customers to send you a sample of their handwriting for a free "one trait analysis" — you will send them, free of charge, only a description of one of their characteristics (e.g., neatness). Very few people will resist the temptation to find out more about themselves after seeing such an example (but be careful not to make it a negative one).

Qualifications needed: Although an official certification is not required in most states, getting one will lend you an air of authority and greatly influence the customer's decision of whether or not to use your services.

Educating yourself: Courses, books, practice.

Number of employees needed to start business (apart from yourself): 0

Things to watch out for: Competition, especially when going after corporate accounts. However, don't forget that your online service will appeal to many people who would never have considered using such a service, and would never have been reached by conventional handwriting analysts.

Additional income: Appearing in courts as an expert witness.

Find a similar business at:
http://myhandwriting.com/

9. DIRECT MAIL SERVICE

Most corporations do not have the personnel and the time to launch a direct mail campaign by themselves. Independent companies do that for them. The services that such a company may perform for its client are:

1. Compiling or buying a mailing list. If it is an e-mail list, make sure the addressees welcome unsolicited messages to their e-mail box.

2. Stuffing envelopes, either by themselves or by employing a sub contractor, and mailing them.

3. Designing and preparing the brochure or sales material that will be sent out to addressees.

Through the Internet, you will enable small and medium companies (or non-profit organizations) to launch their own direct mail campaign from their PCs. They will send you the text for the promotional material or a rough description that you will turn into advertising copy. You will send the final draft for their approval, and upon receiving it proceed to print the number of envelopes agreed upon. You will send them to the names on the list your customer has decided to use (e.g., 50,000 names of people who have donated money to charities during the past year).

The Internet will allow you to work for international entities who want to reach American consumers (for example, newspapers who want to sell subscriptions, or even foreign Internet sites). The key to your success is starting with good mailing lists (which will not be cheap), and the ability to maneuver your clients into combinations that will allow you to give them a better deal (for instance, sending two brochures in one envelope is always cheaper than sending two separate envelopes).

Start-up investment (other than Internet site costs and connection fees): $5,000-$50,000 (most of which will be spent on mailing lists).

International potential: Yes.

Special promotional strategies (in addition to those discussed in chapter 5): Establish links in sites that deal with advertising and promotional services for new businesses. Direct land mail to new businesses. Send press releases to business and trade magazines.

Qualifications needed: None.

Educating yourself: Try to compile as much consumer information and mailing lists as possible. In order to do that you will have to specialize in one pattern of consumers behavior (for example, people who opened up new businesses recently), and dedicate a lot of time to research.

Number of employees needed to start business (apart from yourself): 0-5 (naturally, you will need employees if you decide to handle the envelope stuffing yourself).

Things to watch out for: Make sure the companies you buy the mailing lists from are reputable. Anyone can copy some names from the white pages and call it a mailing list. Buy a sample first (a part of the list you want to purchase), but make sure it is random (e.g., only names beginning with a B) and not comprised of names that the seller himself has chosen for you. Buy the whole list only if this sample proves itself (1.5-2% response is considered good). The postal service and some private companies can show you how to cut down on your postal expenses.

Additional income: Selling mailing lists *you* have compiled to other direct mail companies, or even to list brokers (for more details, see page 88).

Find a similar business at:
http://www.pbdink.com/mail.html

10. INCORPORATION SERVICE

This is one of the easiest businesses to start and operate. All you have to do is order *Certificate of Incorporation* forms for every state you intend to help clients incorporate in (most stationery stores carry them). The forms are quite simple to fill in, but take care to follow their rules to the letter. For example, not placing a comma between the business name and the abbreviation "inc." is reason enough for the state to return the form to you unprocessed. Contact the different states' information services to find out how to fill in these forms. You also have to pay two or three separate fees to the state, and usually order a seal and a stock ledger from a stationery store. For an additional fee, you can also help your customer apply for an Employer Identification Number.

Once you gain experience, the above paperwork can be done in minutes. Add only $50-$100 to your expenses and you will have charged your customers about half of the going rate and a third of what many lawyers with high overhead charge for the same service. This low price and the convenience of setting up a corporation through their computer will make this online service hard to pass up for potential clients.

Using the Internet, you can offer this service nationwide, and even to foreign entities who are interested in setting up a U.S. corporation. All the customer need do is indicate which state they would like to incorporate in and give you the appropriate information (usually the proposed corporation's name, a person to contact and an address). For a fee, you can check the availability of the name of their choice prior to sending the application. This business requires very little time and site maintenance, as well as very little research (after the initial stage) and money investment.

Start-up investment (other than Internet site costs and connection fees): $1,000-$5,000

International potential: Yes.

Special promotional strategies (in addition to those discussed in chapter 5): Link to and from sites that offer services for business or that appeal to the unemployed. Send press releases to business magazines or newspapers that are read by entrepreneurs or the unemployed. An increasing number of unemployed people or frustrated employees who feel trapped in corporate America are trying to set up businesses of their own (particularly from their own homes) rather than rejoin the rat race. Many of them have no prior experience in running a business of their own and they need all the guidance they can get. With these individuals in mind, make sure your site offers information not only on how but also on why businesses should incorporate.

Qualifications needed: None

Educating yourself: Contact local government information centers in different states. Read any books or official leaflets you can find on the subject.

Number of employees needed to start business (apart from yourself): 0

Things to watch out for: Don't be tempted to offer the same price range as conventional incorporating services ($500-$1,000 on average) or customers, preferring the personal touch, will seek *them* out first. Your low price is your greatest asset, so make sure it is prominently displayed in your site.

Additional income: Sell complete incorporation kits — instructions, forms, contact phone numbers and addresses. Offer consultation services through e-mail or chat programs .

Find a similar business at:
http://www.mindspring.com/~dhrobepc

11. ONLINE LITERARY AGENT

This business seems very easy at first glance — all you have to do is collect a few good submissions from writers and sell them to publishers for a 10-15 percent commission, and without having to invest anything but your time. There is a grain of truth in this premise — you will have no trouble finding aspiring writers who would eagerly send you manuscripts of their work. The problem with this business lies with its selling end. True — publishers do tend to give a better viewing chance to novels and book proposals sent by agents, but it might take some time before you make a name for yourself in this business. You have to love this business in order to stay in it long enough for this to happen.

Your site should invite aspiring writers to send samples of their work or query letters by e-mail or FTP files. This will allow you to go over them fast and decide which works you would like to see in full (on average this will probably be no more than 5% of the received submissions). By doing so you will have shortened the time needed to sort through a myriad of manuscripts, and you eliminate paper work and shipping and handling time. The opportunity you give writers to send you samples of their work through e-mail will most certainly lead to your e-mail box overflowing. You may find yourself spending 80-90 percent of your time going through manuscripts you will eventually reject. However, the tremendous number of queries and samples you will receive increases your chances of finding the very good, and more importantly — salable ones. The Internet gives you immediate exposure to tens of thousands of aspiring writers, and makes it easier for them to reach you.

Dealing with publishers is done by land mail, and will probably continue to be done in this manner for years to come. This is the conventional (and hard) side of the business. Now you have to rely on your perseverance and talent for picking winning manuscripts to help you in your struggle to sell your clients' work. This seems hard, but remember that there are thousands of agents who make their living this way (including a few who have become millionaires).

Start-up investment (other than Internet site costs and connection fees): $1,000-$5,000

International potential: Yes.

Special promotional strategies (in addition to those discussed in chapter 5): Getting writers to send you samples of their work is very easy. Just spread the word and they will come. However, make sure you are also listed in literary market guides (e.g., *Writer's Market* or *Insiders' Guide to Book Editors*). Such listings, and press releases to literary magazines, will greatly increase the number of submissions to your agency and convince publishers of your agency's seriousness.

Qualifications needed: You should be able to recognize a good or salable manuscript when you see one.

Educating yourself: Read all the above mentioned guides as well as literary magazines.

Number of employees needed to start business (apart from yourself): 0

Things to watch out for: Spending too much time going over samples or manuscripts you are not going to handle. Specializing and limiting yourself to one or two genres will save you time and make you appear more serious and professional in the eyes of publishers.

Additional income: Offering editing services (but don't make it look like a condition for acceptance or you will make a bad name for yourself).

Find a similar business at:
http://www.literaryagent.com/

12. MORTGAGE LOAN BROKER

In this business — bringing lenders and borrowers together — you will have to tackle various financial problems such as borrowers with insufficient credit history or borrowers who want to take a mortgage with little or no money down.

Your home page will allow you to work with borrowers from all over the U.S., but you must realize that most of them are going to be people who have already exhausted all conventional options. You will probably want to offer your customers not so much low interest rates and low fees as a high approval rate. This means working with flexible lenders and helping your customers get around their financial problems in a variety of ways (e.g., buying mortgage default insurance).

People don't buy a house every day, so it is not likely that many of your customers are going to be repeat customers. However, they may come back to your site several times before reaching the decision to use your services. For this reason, your site must display several articles of useful information that will encourage visitors — some of whom may have already despaired of getting approved for a mortgage — to try again. There is almost always a way to get a mortgage (although not for a low interest rate), and your job is to make people realize it.

Start-up investment (other than Internet site costs and connection fees): $1,000-$2,000

International potential: None.

Special promotional strategies (in addition to those discussed in chapter 5): Link to and from real estate sites. Try to convince them to work with you as a subcontractor. Real estate agents sometimes become frustrated when a client they have spent time and effort on fails to get a mortgage. Your press releases are probably going to be very welcome in magazines and publications that deal with real estate, since your business serves to stimulate the market.

Qualifications needed: Some states require you to get a license in order to operate such a business in their territory.

Educating yourself: Find out everything you can about the mortgage business and related services (such as the above mentioned mortgage default insurance) that would present your customers with several financing options. Subscribe to all related magazines and government publications. Look for workshops, seminars and courses on the subject. You may need to consult a CPA from time to time; for example, when you need information on getting a financial statement for your customers.

Number of employees needed to start business (apart from yourself): 0

Things to watch out for: You need a lot of patience. Some of the harder cases may take many months before they are approved for a mortgage.

Additional income: Selling information packages. Selling advertising space to real estate firms. Charging a referral fee from related businesses (e.g., estimators, CPAs).

Find a similar business at:
http://members.aol.com/ppfllc/ratepg.htm

13. E-MAIL REMINDER SERVICE

This simple, fully automated business will help people organize their lives and avoid getting into trouble — especially with their spouses. Your business, through a mailbot you will set up, will automatically send people e-mail messages to remind them of their spouses' birthdays, of wedding days, business meetings and other important dates. Entering your site, the visitor will be prompted to enter his e-mail address, the date the message is to be sent, and the content of that message (e.g., "Laura's birthday").

There are three possible approaches to this business:

1. Charging your customers for the service, either per message or through a periodical fee that will cover an unlimited number of messages.

2. Making this a free service, but requiring visitors to your site to come back for every reminder they want to set. That way, you have a good chance of attracting as many visitors as the established megasites. This will allow you to sell advertising space at the same rate as they do. With little investment in money and time (the actual reminding is done by special software), you can create one of the Internet's busiest sites.

3. Making this a free service only for users who agree to the

attachment of commercial messages to the reminder they receive through e-mail. Your income is generated both from selling advertising space on your site and from selling (solicited!) direct e-mail advertising. You can also use these commercial messages to promote your own business. For example, if you sell greeting cards, reminding people of special occasions in their life will greatly improve your chances of selling them the appropriate greeting card.

Start-up investment (other than Internet site costs and connection fees): $3,000-$10,000

International potential: Yes.

Special promotional strategies (in addition to those discussed in chapter 5): If the service is free, it is going to be quite easy to promote it through links and newsgroups, and your press releases will probably be of interest to many magazine editors. A good word of mouth promotion is going to be one of the major benefits a free reminder service will bring you. If you intend to charge for the service, try the same methods but expect the response to be on a smaller scale. Business owners and executives are your main target group — establish links to sites they are likely to frequent.

Qualifications needed: None.

Educating yourself: Contact your server service and inquire about the special software you need for your business.

Number of employees needed to start business (apart from yourself): 0

Things to watch out for: You may want to try the first approach — charging for your services — and move on to the other two only if you fail to generate enough income. Remember that capitalizing on the popularity of your site will take time. Don't count on this business to show income for at least a year if you choose to go with the second or third options.

Additional income: Fax-to-e-mail service that will allow people who are not connected to the Internet to send messages/greetings to e-mail addresses.

Find a similar business at:
http://www.gbs.com/flowers/remind.htm

14. ONLINE ADVERTISING AGENCY

Advertising on the Internet is still in its infancy. The number of sites that accept advertising is growing steadily. The number of advertisers is also growing, but there are relatively few services out there whose job it is to put these two groups together. It is hard to find a list of online advertising spaces that includes site usage statistics, ad rates and above all — an overall rating of ad performance on these sites.

This business will give customers just that — an overall view of the online world's advertising opportunities. The customers will learn which of the advertisers offer the best deal for them and which they should stay away from. Statistics will include not only how many hits a site records, but also (whenever possible) what kind of customers visit that site. Your income will be derived from commissions earned on the ads you sell. You can also offer one-on-one consultation services on your site through e-mail or chat programs.

Start-up investment (other than Internet site costs and connection fees): $1,000-$5,000

International potential: Yes.

Special promotional strategies (in addition to those discussed in chapter 5): Establish links in sites that appeal to online entrepreneurs and business owners. Monitor related newsgroups.

Qualifications needed: None.

Educating yourself: Contact as many sites that sell advertising space as you can and negotiate a reasonable commission for yourself in case a client reaches them through your site.

Number of employees needed to start business (apart from yourself): 0

Things to watch out for: Operating this kind of business requires many online hours. You will have to be constantly on the lookout for new advertising spots and changes in existing spots' policies.

Additional income: Online promotion consultant.

Find a similar business at: http://asia-ad.com

15. CUSTOM MADE CALENDARS

The first thing you have do when setting up this type of business is get a good calendar preparation software, a color printer, and a scanner. You should be able to mark special dates on the calendars you sell, such as the customer's birthday. Each page (month) in the calendar should feature a picture or photograph that the customer has either sent you or picked up from a selection displayed in your site. Those customers who choose to send you their own pictures to be put in the custom calendar should be given the opportunity, if they have a scanner, to send them through e-mail. Quick service and high quality will be your greatest assets.

Start-up investment (other than Internet site costs and connection fees): $2,000-$5,000

International potential: Yes.

Special promotional strategies (in addition to those discussed in chapter 5): Send press releases to family oriented magazines. Establish links in sites that deal with families, gifts, holidays.

Qualifications needed: None

Educating yourself: Practice.

Number of employees needed to start business (apart from yourself): 0

Things to watch out for: A message in your site should say specifically that all pictures submitted by conventional mail are to be returned with the calendar. You'll be surprised how many people will be reluctant to use your service for fear of losing their pictures. This is a seasonal business, and the best time of the year for selling calendars is, naturally, October-December.

Additional income: Expanding into similar custom made products: mugs, buttons, pendants, etcetera.

Find a similar business at:
http://www.multi-ad.com/CMR/calndars.html

16. CLIP ART/STOCK PHOTOGRAPHY SERVICE

One huge advantage of operating this kind of business online is the elimination of the need for costly catalogs. This reduces the necessary start up investment to about half that of the equivalent conventional business. Your site is your catalog. For this reason, it has to be huge. The success of any clip art /stock photography business depends on the variety it offers its customers, and this means at least several hundred images that your site will have to display for visitors.

Your customers are advertising agencies, promoters, corporations who are about to print a brochure, and anyone else who needs artwork or a photograph but cannot afford to hire an in-house artist or photographer. They will look for a specific kind of image, and therefore the images in your site must be arranged by subject matter and be reachable through a user friendly menu. It is a good idea to show visitors very small, fast appearing pictures first. If the customer likes any of these tiny pictures she will click on it to view the full-size, slower appearing picture.

The site can be fully automated, wherein the customer downloads the image she chooses, or manual, where you mail the selected image to her. Either way, the main chunk of the work you will have to put into your business will go to setting up your huge site and scanning all your images into it.

You can obtain the artworks or photographs from four sources:

1. Freelance artists or photographers who will work on a fee or commission basis. Many beginners will be delighted to have their work displayed in your site, especially when there is a real chance of them being sold.

2. By working in collaboration with, or as an agent of, other stock photographers (especially conventional).

3. By purchasing your images from the artist/photographer or from other stock photographers. This is not recommended unless you are certain that the image is salable.

4. Creating them yourself. If you are a photographer or an artist you can save yourself a lot of money and trouble. Try to concentrate on the subjects that are most in demand; for example, hi-tech images (electronic circuits, communication equipment, computer designs).

Start-up investment (other than Internet site costs and connection fees): $1,000-$100,000

International potential: Yes.

Special promotional strategies (in addition to those discussed in chapter 5): Invite everyone, not just potential customers, to visit your site, which will thus become a free online exhibition. The number of visitors will increase, and even if only a small percentage of these turn out to be actual customers, their number will grow over time. To start building up your image bank, search for all the magazines that beginning artists or photographers are likely to read and send your press releases or place your ads there.

Qualifications needed: Photographic or artistic skill is a major plus in this business.

Educating yourself: Learn what is in demand in today's market; what kind of images your customers are looking for.

Number of employees needed to start business (apart from yourself): 0

Things to watch out for: You may need to constantly change and add to the variety of images in your site until you find out what your customers want. Your online presence may be costly — this is, after all, a large site.

Additional income: If you make a name for your site as an online free museum, you can start selling advertising space.

Find a similar business at: http://www.photodisc.com

17. CREDIT CARD CONSULTANT

It is relatively easy to get a credit card nowadays, and lenders are often accused of having too lax approval standards. In light of this, it is amazing to learn that so many people do not know how to get a credit card, or that they believe that they can never apply for one again because of past financial problems.

There are many ways for people with no credit history or even those who have gone through bankruptcies to get a credit card. There are secured credit cards, which require the holder to deposit a collateral with the issuing company equal to or larger than the card's credit limit. Although the only immediate advantage that such a card will give a person is the ability to order products through the telephone or online, this *is* the first step in rebuilding a credit record. In most cases, six months to one year after the issuing of the secured card, the customer may apply for a "real", unsecured card (provided they kept a good credit record during that time).

There are other ways to help people with credit problems to get back on their feet, and it is your site's job to make these people aware of them. You can offer them the following services:

1. One on one consultation (through e-mail or chat programs).

2. Selling information packages, including addresses of credit card issuing banks. This can be done immediately through e-mail or by conventional mail.

3. Acting on the customer's behalf. You fill in all the forms (which they need only sign), send them to the right places and work with the customer until he receives his credit card through the mail. For you, after a while, this will be a simple enough process, but people who are confused and overwhelmed by the financial hurdles they face will greatly appreciate it.

Credit card consulting on the Internet has its pros and cons. On the one hand, the percentage of your potential customers (people with credit problems) in the online world is smaller than the general population's average. On the other hand, a great number of Internet users are students (using their institutes' Internet access rather than their own computers), who are in dire need of credit. Also, unlike your conventional counterparts, you have a nationwide appeal.

Start-up investment (other than Internet site costs and connection fees): $1,000-$5,000

International potential: None.

Special promotional strategies (in addition to those discussed in chapter 5): Establish links in sites that students are likely to visit. Send press releases to publications and magazines students are likely to read, as well as regional, general interest and consumer magazines.

Qualifications needed: None.

Educating yourself: Directories, publications. Compile a list of secured credit card issuers. Read all you can about the subject and go to seminars and workshops.

Number of employees needed to start business (apart from yourself): 0

Things to watch out for: Some people, especially those who have gone through bankruptcies only recently, will be turned down even for a secured credit card. Be straightforward about it, and don't waste your time and theirs.

Additional income: Expand into other types of credit lines or loans. For example, you can help customers with financial problems to get a second mortgage or a car loan.

Find a similar business at:
http://www.tdbank.ca/tdbank/Creditctr/prodinfo/prodinfo.html

18. ONLINE FREELANCE WRITER

There are two different faces to this business: writing for magazines and writing for businesses. Although the first would be the one to bring you the fame and prestige, it its usually the latter that you will have to rely on for income.

A large number of magazines and newspapers accept submissions through e-mail, and this number is steadily growing. It is easier for editors to browse through their e-mail boxes and select the few articles they need than it is for them to open and sort hundreds of letters. For the freelance writer the advantages are even more significant: the process of submitting articles to magazines is speeded up considerably, and mail/stationery expenses are eliminated.

Most small magazines do not pay much ($50-500) for an article, and even so, it is not easy to get your article accepted. Editors receive a tremendous number of submissions, and in order to stand out from all the rest your article has to be both well written and of interest to the magazine's readers. The larger the magazine (in circulation terms) the harder it will be to get your submission accepted. It is better, of course, if you concentrate on a subject you know.

Unless you are very good at it (or you are a celebrity), don't count on newspapers and magazines to put your children through college. Publishing articles in magazines should be counted on only as a way to build up prestige. It is this prestige that will allow you to better market your other service — writing for corporations.

Corporations need writers for a variety of projects: brochures, press releases, presentations, even speeches. You site must appeal to small businesses, who are more likely to use your services at first, as well as to larger corporations that you hope to hook eventually. Show your credentials: your home page must display your prior publishing record: businesses you have written for and, more importantly, magazines who have published your articles. If you specialize in one or two subjects, your customers should be made aware of any experience you have in those areas. Include a few samples of your writing in your site.

Start-up investment (other than Internet site costs and connection fees): $1,000-$5,000

International potential: Yes.

Special promotional strategies (in addition to those discussed in chapter 5): Referrals will account for much of your business, so try to get word of mouth going by making your site an attraction. For example, you can offer a few well written articles for free downloading and use (these, of course, will have to be articles of a general nature, such as reports on the growth of a certain industry and predictions for its future). Establish links in sites that offer services for businesses or ones that deal with promotion and advertising.

Qualifications needed: Writing skills.

Educating yourself: Other than building up your writing skills, you should also compile a list of magazines and newspapers that accept submissions by e-mail..

Number of employees needed to start business (apart from yourself): 0

Things to watch out for: It may be some time before you make a name for yourself. It is better not to rely on this business for reasonable income for at least a year or two.

Additional income: Other services for businesses, such as editing important letters or preparing sales material (especially for exhibitions, trade shows, etcetera).

Find a similar business at:
http://www.mv.com/ipusers/lorvig/writer/writer.htm

19. HERB GROWING

Unlike other crops, herb growing requires very little space; so small, in fact, that even a large basement might suffice for this purpose. It is an easy, fun and relaxing business that, while not making you a millionaire, can produce a good income. Your customers will include restaurants, health food stores and of course individuals. The low shipping costs and the fact that this business requires only a few hours a week to operate make this an ideal online business. You have to spend very little on inventory (mostly seeds), and although it will do your business no harm, you don't need to display photographs of your products in your site.

Start-up investment (other than Internet site costs and connection fees): $3,000-$10,000

International potential: Yes (some countries may have custom regulations and import restrictions that you have to take into account, though).

Special promotional strategies (in addition to those discussed in chapter 5): Establish links in sites that deal with nutrition, exotic foods, diet, lifestyles, tourism, hobbies (especially cooking). Send press releases to magazines that deal with the same subjects. Your site should offer as much information about the herbs you sell as possible, as well as general information about nutrition and health. Educate your customers — this is the kind of business that draws only educated consumers; no one will buy herbs unless they know something about them.

Qualifications needed: None, although a background in agriculture will significantly shorten the initial period of experimentations.

Educating yourself: Read and learn everything you can about the subject. Start practicing at least several months before you open your business.

Number of employees needed to start business (apart from yourself): 0

Things to watch out for: Lots of competition. Try to offer "new discoveries" in addition to the traditional or "in" herbs.

Additional income: Sell info packages on how to grow herbs to those who are interested in it. True, you may be creating more competition for your business this way, but then, people who are interested in growing their own herbs would buy books on the subject anyway. At least be the one who sells these books to them.

Find a similar business at: http://www.richters.com

20. ONLINE EMPLOYMENT AGENCY

Surf the Internet and you will find that many sites, especially those which serve as an online front to large corporations, display a "job/career opportunities" option that, when clicked on, leads the visitor to a list of current openings in the company. You can compile a list of these sites and utilize this information in three ways:

1. Sell the list/links to the public for a fixed fee.

2. Use it to help individuals find employment. You will have to contact the employers yourself and negotiate a fee with them prior to representing them. This is not unlike the function of a conventional employment agency.

3. Allow visitors to your site free access to those links. This is the "heavy-traffic" approach, where your income comes from other services (résumé writing, one on one consultation, selling info packages) and from accepting advertising.

Whichever option you choose, you can also combine some of the methods of a conventional employment agency. In other words, don't shun conventional sources such as newspaper ads to help you place employees.

Start-up investment (other than Internet site costs and connection fees): $1,000-$5,000

International potential: Yes (but you have to specialize in this field and be familiar with different countries' working visas and laws for foreign employees).

Special promotional strategies (in addition to those discussed in chapter 5): Establish links in sites that attract unemployed people; for example, those which offer ways to save money on everyday products. Send press releases to magazines and newspapers of almost all classifications since this business is of a general appeal.

Qualifications needed: None.

Educating yourself: Know how to write a résumé, how to assess job applicants, and find out what different employers are looking for in a new employee.

Number of employees needed to start business (apart from yourself): 0

Things to watch out for: Some of the job searchers you will represent might turn out to be prima-donnas — they would turn down any job if it doesn't bring the title "manager" along with it, for instance. Other applicants might have unrealistic expectations about health care benefits. You can find yourself spending an unproportionately long time with such individuals.

Additional income: Résumé writing service.

Find a similar business at: http://www.recruiting-links.com

21. RÉSUMÉ WRITING SERVICE

Unfortunately, a well written résumé can mean the difference between being hired and moving on to the next job application. Most people can list their former employers and their qualifications easily enough, but not having seen too many résumés in their lives, they will probably not know how to make their own résumé stand out from dozens of others. Your job is first to collect every relevant piece of information from your customer, and then to put it in a dynamic, effective form. Your Internet site can do the first part for you. The customer will fill in a form, either through e-mail or by answering a questionnaire built into your site. You will then turn this into a résumé, and either send a number of copies (printed on high quality paper) to him by mail or else send it through e-mail (an increasing number of people send their résumés through e-mail).

Your main task is to convince visitors to your site to use your services. For this reason you have to give them samples of your work ("before" and "after" texts for instance) and offer as much information as possible about the importance of a well written résumé in today's job market.

Start-up investment (other than Internet site costs and connection fees): $1,000-$5,000

International potential: Yes, for foreign nationals wishing to work in the U.S.

Special promotional strategies (in addition to those discussed in chapter 5): Establishing links in sites that appeal to job searchers is a must. Try to work on a pay-by-referral basis with employment agencies (online and conventional).

Qualifications needed: Writing skills.

Educating yourself: Study well written résumés and note the changes in style in accordance with the applicants' profession and qualifications. Learn all you can about employers in today's business world and what they are looking for in an employee.

Number of employees needed to start business (apart from yourself): 0

Things to watch out for: Take care not to hype-up your résumés too much. This may be frowned upon and viewed as an attempt to cover up the fact that the applicant has actually nothing to say. You will probably have to offer low prices or good deals (e.g., 500 high-quality copies included in the price) to compete with the large number of similar businesses out there.

Additional income: Sell packages of winner-résumés — a collection of about a hundred well written résumés to help those of your site's visitors who will want to phrase their own résumé.

Find a similar business at:
http://holmes.law.cwru.edu/cwrulaw/career/resume.html

22. ONLINE TRANSLATION SERVICE

Two main services can be performed by this online business:

1. Conventional translation of documents and letters. The customers who visit your site send you the document, whether by fax or (better) e-mail, and you e-mail them the translated text as quickly as possible. You can charge for this service either by the hour or by the size and number of the documents. This is a very convenient service for corporations who receive letters written in foreign languages, or who need to write such letters.

2. Translation of online text. English speaking countries still comprise the majority of the online world, but this may not last forever. Even today there are many sites without as much as one English word written in them. When an American businessman, for example, wants to view information on one of these sites or contact its Webmaster, he needs to rely on the services of a

translator. This problem applies both ways — for instance, when a Japanese businessman needs to interact with an American corporation's site and finds out that he can't. The online translation service gives them the opportunity to view or interact with foreign language sites without the need to summon a translator to their office in person.

Your customers will tell you which site they are interested in, and you will visit that site and send them its translated text through e-mail. If they wish to contact the sites' Webmaster, you can write and send an e-mail message for them.

Start-up investment (other than Internet site costs and connection fees): $1,000-$5,000

International potential: Yes.

Special promotional strategies (in addition to those discussed in chapter 5): If you go with the second service, most, if not all of your customers will be corporations who need to deal with foreign companies. Establish links in sites that offer services for businesses. Press releases are very important and should be sent not only to U.S. business and trade magazines but also to their foreign counterparts (whose language you cover in your translation service). Some nations are known for lack of linguistic skills, and their people speak no foreign languages. Find the sites or land addresses of these countries' businesses, and offer your services through direct mail. Some of them might have in-house translators, but definitely not all.

Qualifications needed: A mastery of the foreign languages you intend to translate.

Educating yourself: Some languages are more in demand then others, of course. Speaking fluent Japanese, for instance, is certain to get you places in this business.

Number of employees needed to start business (apart from yourself): 0 (unless you want your services to cover more languages than you yourself speak).

Things to watch out for: Certain phrases in foreign languages won't transcend the cultural boundary by conventional translation, and may mislead your customer. You must tell them when a sentence or a word is ambiguous in order not to be accused later of providing a false translation.

Additional income: Having helped to initiate business relations between two parties, you may also want to become an interpreter in real time voice conversations (between them) for an additional fee (see also: ONLINE INTERPRETER, page 182).

Find a similar business at:
http://www.lec.com/transserv/transserv_acct_form.html

23. WEB SITE DESIGNER

Fees for this service have gone down significantly due to high competition and the availability of home page designer software that allow even people with no knowledge of HTML to create their own home pages.

Still, the market is large enough and continually growing, and with the new software you too can work faster and possibly maintain the same working-time-per-dollar ratio of previous years. You can offer your clients the following services:

1. Designing a Web site form A to Z — you design the graphics, the layout, the features, and then convert it all to HTML.

2. Taking an already designed Web site layout (either in detail or as a rough layout) and converting it to HTML.

3. Improving on existing sites (adding online features and so on).

Start-up investment (other than Internet site costs and connection fees): $1,000-$5,000

International potential: Yes.

Special promotional strategies (in addition to those discussed in chapter 5): There are thousands of similar businesses out there; if you want magazines or a newspapers to publish your press releases you will have to make your site unique. Turn your site into a center for free information (for new Internet subscribers/businesses) for example, and promote it as such. Consider combining this service with related services such as one on one online consultation.

Qualifications needed: None.

Educating yourself: Learn HTML and Java. View as many Web sites as possible and pick up some good design ideas.

Number of employees needed to start business (apart from yourself): 0

Things to watch out for: Lots of competition. Not every system (for example: non-Internet networks) can support all Web features.

Additional income: In addition to the graphic and HTML designing of the site itself, you can also write the text content for an additional fee. For this you will need good communicative and language skills and a knack for marketing and promotion.

Find a similar business at: There are literally thousands of these. Use a search engine to locate them.

24. ONLINE DATING SERVICE

There are several ways to go about this:

1. A traditional dating service model. You will create a special file for each of your clients, similar in appearance to a home page, which will present the client's picture, a short description and any message he or she may want to leave. Acting as a matchmaker, you will then make these files accessible to the right person, who will then decide whether or not to contact the other person.

2. Turn your site into a classified-ads board. For a fee, every client will be able to leave a file similar to the one described above, and this file will be displayed in your site for a predetermined period of time. The difference between this and the first approach lies in the accessibility of these files — here they can be accessed by *any* visitor to your site. To make this process more efficient, you can use a database to help visitors find the matches they are interested in by using certain keywords (e.g., female, non-smoker, likes swimming, professional, 40+). This type of business is fully automated, and your only job will be the scanning of clients' photos into their files.

3. A service similar to the above option, with the exception that it is the visitor to the site who has to pay rather than the people who are registered with it. This will probably ensure a greater client base, but will also restrict the number of visitors.

Start-up investment (other than Internet site costs and connection fees): $5,000-$15,000

International potential: Yes. However, you will have to establish more sites to deal with different geographical areas.

Special promotional strategies (in addition to those discussed in chapter 5): Send press releases to singles magazines. Link to and from sites that appeal to singles.

Qualifications needed: None, but good communicative skills will most certainly help you.

Number of employees needed to start business (apart from yourself): 0

Things to watch out for: Unless this was your original intention, don't let your site deteriorate into a sleazy online joint. This will deter serious clients. Reserve the right to reject any customer file that is not up to your standards.

Additional income: For an additional fee, you can offer your customers help in preparing their online presentation. You can give them advice on phrasing their message in a dynamic way and on the right photograph or video file to attach to it (e.g., what to wear for it).

Find a similar business at:http://www.1st-site.com/

25. E-MAIL TO FAX/FAX TO E-MAIL SERVICE

This simple-to-operate business provides the link between the conventional and the online worlds. For example, let us assume that someone without Internet access (over 95% of the world's population still belong in this group!) wants to contact another person through e-mail. They call or send a fax to your business, and you turn their message into an e-mail message and send it to its designated online destination.

Another, perhaps more important service you can provide is doing just the opposite — turning e-mail messages into faxes. Why should anyone want to do this? For one, they may not have a fax machine. Most Internet users are either students or individuals. Also, they may wish to send faxes while traveling (through Internet connections other than their own) or they may wish to send lengthy faxes from abroad, maybe even to several people, and save on telecommunication charges.

Start-up investment (other than Internet site costs and connection fees): $1,000-$5,000

International potential: Yes.

Special promotional strategies (in addition to those discussed in chapter 5): Your promotion has to appeal both to the online and to the conventional crowds. Press releases (especially to business, trade and career/college magazines) are your greatest promotional tool. Establish links in sites that are likely to be frequented by students and executives.

Qualifications needed: None.

Number of employees needed to start business (apart from yourself): 0

Things to watch out for: When setting your fees, don't forget to take into account long-distance calls.

Additional income: Your business can also offer an e-mail-to-voice service, where you will receive e-mail messages for a certain person (without an Internet access) and immediately contact that person by telephone. This can be a great tool for businessmen who need to contact traveling executives, or who would like to leave an immediate message to several people and do not have the time to call them individually. It can also come in handy when contacting a visually impaired person.

Find a similar business at:
http://www.faxaway.com/

26. ONLINE CUSTOM MADE GIFT BASKETS

This business, which has traditionally been based on mail and catalog orders, takes another step forward with the advent of the Internet, and allows clients to custom design their own gift baskets.

Your site will give the visitor two choices:

1. Choosing from a selection of several "mass-produced" gift basket designs. The customer will be shown photographs of the baskets together with a short description of their contents.

2. Putting together their own basket. The customers are presented with a menu of several items (especially food items), preferably with small photographs attached (not too large, so as not to force the customer to move between several Web pages). The customers pick the items they wish to place in their baskets (e.g., different kinds of wine, candy or decorations) and their quantity. When they are done, your site will automatically compute and display the total price for the package the customer has put together. This price has to be slightly higher than that of the mass-produced baskets, naturally. What you will need to receive through your site is a list of the items that are to be put into the customers' baskets, and of course their address and billing information.

Start-up investment (other than Internet site costs and connection fees): $5,000-$20,000

International potential: None.

Special promotional strategies (in addition to those discussed in chapter 5): This product is of a general appeal. As conventional competition is high, try to concentrate on online promotion. Establish links in sites that deal with gifts and holidays. When sending press releases, direct the editors' attention to the self planning feature of your site or it will not stand out from hundreds of similar businesses.

Qualifications needed: None.

Educating yourself: Study your competitors' best designed and decorated gift baskets. Practice.

Number of employees needed to start business (apart from yourself): 0

Things to watch out for: Although the items you put in the basket have to be inexpensive to lower costs, make sure this does not come before quality. Repeat customers are your greatest asset. This is an easy, yet highly competitive business, where you must have a unique product or approach.

Additional income: A very natural step for this type of business will be to expand into flower arrangements and other gifts.

Find a similar business at:
http://www.olworld.com/olworld/m_silverelephantz

27. ONLINE GREETING CARDS

Visitors to the Internet site of such a business will find a selection of greeting cards they can choose from. They should have at least three options:

1. Choosing an "as-is" card from the selection, with a fixed message (e.g., *Season's Greetings*). You will then send the card of their choice to the address they supply you with.

2. Customizing their own card. This will include inserting their own message onto the card they choose or even custom designing their own card using your site's image bank. This will

require you to print the cards yourself and will incur additional costs.

3. Setting up an account with your business. This is a good idea for medium to large corporations. They will only have to forward the list of addressees to you, give instructions as to which cards to send out to whom on what occasions, and leave all the year round trouble of carrying it out in a timely and organized fashion to you.

Start-up investment (other than Internet site costs and connection fees): $5,000-$20,000

International potential: Yes.

Special promotional strategies (in addition to those discussed in chapter 5): Establish links in sites that deal with gifts and gift ideas, holidays, personal services, services for businesses. Press releases must be timed so that they appear shortly before the holiday season.

Qualifications needed: None.

Educating yourself: Find out which cards are most in demand. Try to come up with new catchy ideas since originality and creativity count in this business.

Number of employees needed to start business (apart from yourself): 0

Things to watch out for: Competition. Don't base your site entirely on your original ideas until they prove salable — keep some of the classic, proven cards as well. Make sure you have an adequate stock of any one card before you scan its image into your site, since you may find it difficult to order new cards during the holiday season. Basically, this is a seasonal business, but birthdays and other special occasions in people's lives will carry you through the slower parts of the year.

Additional income: Since mailing costs for greeting cards are very low, this is an ideal international business. If you offer a choice of several languages in your site, in addition to a few cards that feature themes from foreign countries' culture and holidays, you can expand your market significantly.

Find a similar business at: http://www.valentine.com

28. SEARCH SERVICE

Are online search engines doing a good job at finding information? If the subject you are looking for is "Ancient Rome" you will no doubt find numerous articles about it. If, however, you need to find out the reasons for the battle between Aetius and Boniface at Rimini, the user's job is going to be much harder and will require a long, possibly off-line search.

Researching is not easy. You need to know something about the subject you are searching for. In the above example, a certain knowledge of Ancient Roman history will shorten your search time considerably. Also, you will have to rely on resources outside the Internet, and will no doubt make many trips to the library. Most of your customers will probably be businesses that need to find information about a certain company, product, legislation, dates or people. Another group of potential customers is students, who will need your help to complete their assignments.

Charging by the hour is of course ideal for you, but it may not attract too many customers during the first stage of your business existence. Try to offer a per-assignment fee instead. This will require you to estimate the research time for every subject as accurately as possible.

Start-up investment (other than Internet site costs and connection fees): $1,000-$5,000

International potential: Yes.

Special promotional strategies (in addition to those discussed in chapter 5): List your business in all the directories search engines are listed in. In the short description of your business that accompanies such listings, include a line such as "If you couldn't find it anywhere else — we'll find it for you!" Establish links in sites that attract both students (be prepared to offer them a low fee) and executives.

Qualifications needed: You must be able to organize data and to have enough general knowledge to be able to narrow down your search to the right area as quickly as possible.

Educating yourself: Practice online search. Compile a list of online and off-line directories and databases.

Number of employees needed to start business (apart from yourself): 0

Things to watch out for: Taking on assignments which are not within your field of expertise.

Additional income: Turn your site into a search center, with links to many other search services — not just the big search engines. If this site is user-friendly enough, it is possible that some Internet users will set it as the first page in their browsers. Just like the bigger search engines, you will then be able to accept advertising.

Find a similar business at: http://www.trademarkinfo.com/

29. TONER CARTRIDGE REMANUFACTURING

Toner cartridges for laser printers are very expensive. With a price range of $70-$140, they rarely last for more than 4,000 pages. Businesses are especially hard hit by these expenses, and pay anything between several hundreds to several thousands a year for replacing used cartridges. Refilling kits or compatible toner cartridges sell on the market for a lot less and achieve the same result as a new cartridge.

Anyone who owns a laser printer has a computer as well. Computer owners can have access to the Internet, and a great many of them are therefore present in the online world. For this reason, this type of business seems to have been made for the Internet. Your site can offer your customers three basic options:

1. Buying a remanufactured (by you) cartridge (they sell for about 50-70 percent of a new cartridge price).

2. Buying a compatible toner cartridge or a refilling kit.

3. Exchanging their used cartridges (provided you need them at the time) for a discount on remanufactured ones.

Start-up investment (other than Internet site costs and connection fees): $1,000-$10,000

International potential: Only for selling kits. The shipping costs for heavy laser printer cartridges can easily offset the difference between a remanufactured cartridge and a new one.

Special promotional strategies (in addition to those discussed in chapter 5): This is a business of general appeal, so concentrate on establishing as many links and directory listings as possible. Offer additional, free services in your site to attract visitors (e.g., FAQs about laser printer maintenance, troubleshooting files, review and rating of printer models).

Qualifications needed: None.

Educating yourself: This is a very easy business to learn, but make sure you practice on different cartridge models before you go online.

Number of employees needed to start business (apart from yourself): 0

Things to watch out for: Shipping costs.

Additional income: You can expand into refilling copy machine cartridges.

Find a similar business at: http://www.laserflex.com/

30. RUBBER STAMP MANUFACTURER

This is another business that seems to have been born for the Internet. Your customers will be presented with a selection of several stamp types (e.g., self-inking stamps) and sizes to choose from. Selecting the type and size of the font they need, your customers will then key in the text of the stamp, and their address. The whole process must be made very simple and fast for the customer, and the ordered stamps should be shipped out to her as quickly as possible. This is a very easy business that requires only a small investment and a very small inventory, but allows for a high margin of profit.

Start-up investment (other than Internet site costs and connection fees): $2,000-$10,000

International potential: Small (shipping expenses will make it hard to compete with foreign stamp manufacturers).

Special promotional strategies (in addition to those discussed in chapter 5): You have to think of ways to stimulate magazine editors to take interest in your site and publish your press releases. Consider offering additional (preferably free) services in your site to achieve this purpose. Establish links in sites that offer services for businesses.

Qualifications needed: None.

Number of employees needed to start business (apart from yourself): 0

Things to watch out for:
Competition. Your one disadvantage is that your business cannot offer rush, same day service. However, very few people need a rubber stamp in a matter of hours, and as long as you keep delivery time to a minimum, this will not be a serious problem.

Additional income: It is only natural for this type of business to make corporate seals or sell products such as price marking guns.

Find a similar business at:
http://www.inficad.com/~kady/

31. TAX PREPARATION SERVICE

The key problem in this potentially high income business is how to make your site user friendly and yet as fully automated as possible. People who use tax preparation services do so either because they do not understand the I.R.S. guidelines or because they simply don't have the time to organize their financial data and fill in all the necessary forms.

Your clients will send you, through various online forms that your site will support (or fax, if they prefer to), all the information you need to fill in their forms for them. However, take into account a certain amount of one-on-one conversation with them, either by e-mail or chat programs. Tax preparation is not meant for everyone. It involves a tremendous amount of paperwork, computations and attention to detail, and you must really love all those things in order to be a success in this business.

Start-up investment (other than Internet site costs and connection fees): $2,000-$10,000

International potential: None.

Special promotional strategies (in addition to those discussed in chapter 5): As this is a seasonal business, concentrate your promotional efforts during the right time of the year. Your customers are individuals, not businesses and probably not students. Make sure you are registered in every possible search engine and directory, and try to give your site a unique edge in order to impress magazine editors. For example, you could offer some free service or access to free information to pull in the crowds.

Qualifications needed: None, unless you want to offer additional tax services and become a CPA.

Educating yourself: Courses, seminars, books, workshops are a must. You will also have to purchase special accounting software.

Number of employees needed to start business (apart from yourself): 0

Things to watch out for. Get the right errors/omissions insurance.

Additional income: Any other accounting or bookkeeping services. Online financial consultant.

Find a similar business at:http://members.aol.com/preparetax/

32. ONLINE TYPESETTER

Typesetters take formless text and turn it into typeset copies ready to be transferred to printer's plates. Although typesetters sometimes handle book-length manuscripts, most of your work will be preparing brochures, sales material, newsletters and other short-length printed material. Competition in the software industry has made it possible today to purchase an excellent desktop publishing software for a few hundred dollars. High grade laser printers sell for as low as $400-$500 today. Customers no longer pay you for the expensive equipment and software you use, but for your time and skill.

An online typesetting site will save your customers time and effort. They will be able to transfer their text to you by e-mail (or fax, if they prefer to), and attach instructions for typesetting it (font size, page size, images and graphics). However, you may still need to rely on one-on-one conversations through online chat programs to work out some of the fine details. The finished product can either be mailed out to the customer or converted into files that can be downloaded by her (e.g., Corel 7 or compatible files).

Start-up investment (other than Internet site costs and connection fees): $5,000-$10,000

International potential: Yes.

Special promotional strategies (in addition to those discussed in chapter 5): Establish links in sites that offer services for businesses (especially new businesses). Search for potential online customers and send them direct mail (to their land address, which you can find on their Web site, not to their e-mail address).

Qualifications needed: None, but you need to develop a good eye for text layout and learn how to creatively utilize all the features of desktop publishing software.

Educating yourself: Courses, seminars, lots of practice.

Number of employees needed to start business (apart from yourself): 0

Things to watch out for: Since you will charge by assignment rather than by the hour it is important to correctly estimate the time you will need to spend on each job.

Additional income: Putting together a complete publishing package: you use subcontractors (printers, artists, delivery service) in order to give the customer the finished product: books, brochures, leaflets, etc.

Find a similar business at:
http://www.eisenbrauns.com/typesetting.html

33. CUSTOM PRINTED PRODUCTS

Mugs, T-shirts, sweatshirts, key chains, buttons — all these and many other products can have a photograph attached to them, either by digital or conventional means. Most of the machinery needed for transferring images onto product do not come cheap, but the investment is still smaller than what is required to start up a one hour photo lab. If you can't afford such an investment, try to start out by offering only one or two products — a basic printer for T-shirts, for example, can be purchased for just several hundred dollars.

You can offer your customers two types of products:

1. Ready made products. The customer views the selection displayed in your site and chooses the product with the image (logos, cartoons) they like most. You don't need any equipment for these kinds of products if you decide to purchase them from a wholesaler, but then you will not be able to offer your own unique product line.

2. Custom printed products. The customer sends you a photo or an image, either through e-mail attachments or land mail, and then selects from your site the product she wants the image to be printed on.

Start-up investment (other than Internet site costs and connection fees): $15,000-$50,000

International potential: Yes.

Special promotional strategies (in addition to those discussed in chapter 5): Press releases for this business will probably get the editors' attention only if you offer a unique, appealing line of products or a revolutionary new idea. Establish links in sites that deal with gifts, clothing (for T-shirts), photography.

Qualifications needed: None.

Educating yourself: Training will probably be offered by the machine manufacturers themselves, and then — practice, practice, practice.

Number of employees needed to start business (apart from yourself): 0

Things to watch out for: Some of the new digital imaging machines will cost you an arm and a leg while offering only a slight improvement over their yesteryear predecessors. Purchasing a used machine — a three or four year old model — might prove a better business decision in the long run, and may save you from committing to a long, costly lease.

Additional income: You can expand into posters, photo retouching and even marketing your best selling line of products through a national distributor. It will also be a natural step for you to sell other lines of gifts in your site, such as toys, games, decorative items, frames, china, and housewares.

Find a similar business at:
http://www.netins.net/showcase/kinnes/

34. ONLINE IMPORT/EXPORT CONSULTANT

Import and export regulations are often a deterring factor that causes business owners to forgo business deals. These regulations vary from one country to the other: some products are allowed to be shipped to any foreign destination while others require licensing; customs duties may be imposed on certain goods from some countries, while other goods from different countries would be allowed in free of any tariffs.

Business people often find themselves overwhelmed and confused by the complexity of the task at had. In most cases, all they need is consultation, a few rules made clear. At other times, they may need a professional to fill in forms for them or to take care of the entire process of importing/exporting their products. An Internet site that will help business people with this problem will be greatly appreciated.

Your site can be created as an information center, and display FAQs and related articles. You can also sell related literature or information packages, and provide consultation services through e-mail, chat programs or conventional means.

Start-up investment (other than Internet site costs and connection fees): $1,000-$5,000

International potential: Yes.

Special promotional strategies (in addition to those discussed in chapter 5): With the online world's ongoing population explosion, more and more small businesses that previously catered only to local markets find themselves having to deal with international (online) trade. There is a good chance that many of them will be looking for you. However, you can increase your chances by registering your business with every possible search engine and directory, by establishing links in other sites dedicated to business services and consultation, and by keeping an eye on the right newsgroups. Press releases should be directed not only to business magazines but also to magazines of a more general nature that small business owners are likely to read.

Qualifications needed: A background in foreign trade will be helpful.

Educating yourself: Courses, seminars, and of course every relevant government (U.S. and foreign) publication you can lay a hand on.

Number of employees needed to start business (apart from yourself): 0

Things to watch out for: You have to be constantly on the lookout for new import/export regulations.

Additional income: Additional business consultation services. Partnerships in foreign trade deals.

Find a similar business at:
http://www.briscdisc.co.za/exserve/index.html

35. ONLINE TICKET AGENCY

For this type of business, which has traditionally been associated with 800 numbers and phone orders, setting up an Internet site is a very natural step. It is one of the simplest sites to create: no graphics are necessary (except, maybe, for the home page), and a simple menu will be enough to lead your customers to the event of their choice. The variety of events you can sell tickets to is huge — sport events, concerts, musicals, operas, theater, Christmas shows and many others.

Aside from selling tickets, your site must offer information about events, ticket prices (including group discounts) and availability. Welcome corporate accounts and offer written confirmation of seats.

Your customers are not the only ones you are going to deal with online — the ticket distribution centers you have to work with can also be reached there.

Start-up investment (other than Internet site costs and connection fees): $5,000-$20,000

International potential: Yes (for tourists about to arrive in the U.S.).

Special promotional strategies (in addition to those discussed in chapter 5): Send press releases to magazines that specialize in entertainment — sports, movies, classical music. Establish links in sites that deal with these subjects. Monitor relevant newsgroups.

Qualifications needed: A licence is required in most states.

Educating yourself: The best way to learn this business is to work for a ticket agency for a few months. Consult CPAs (this business involves a lot of accounting) and government organizations aimed at helping small businesses.

Number of employees needed to start business (apart from yourself): 0

Things to watch out for: Competing with the large ticket agencies is not easy, and making a name for yourself in this business will take some time. Many of your customers will expect next day delivery of the tickets.

Additional income: Tourist information and services. Restaurant referral service.

Find a similar business at:
http://www.vnm.com/musicalchairs

36. HOME MADE FOOD ITEMS

Exotic drinks, delicacies, special desserts, ethnic food, gourmet items, — these are food items that are rarely found in supermarkets or groceries. Even delicatessens or gourmet shops do not sell more than a few kinds of these food items — and the potential variety is limitless.

This is an easy business, but you are required to do at least these two things to ensure its success:

1. Find out which food items are in demand, trendy or hard to get.

2. Learn how to make these items well — you will need a solid base of repeat customers to rely on.

Place high quality photographs of your products in your site. A detailed description of each item, together with a list of ingredients, will be greatly appreciated. Make sure your site does not neglect different consumer groups, such as vegetarians. An important consumer group you should acknowledge are the adventurers. They are looking for new gastronomic experiences and the only reason they will visit your site will be to look for new things they have not yet tried. For this (quite large) group, make sure your site displays at least one or two exotic, relatively unknown items that will be changed once a month.

Start-up investment (other than Internet site costs and connection fees): $1,000-$5,000

International potential: Yes. However, many countries ban the import of food items without proper licensing.

Special promotional strategies (in addition to those discussed in chapter 5): Word of mouth will promote this type of business more than anything else. Attracting the first customers to your site will be just a small hurdle; making sure they remain as repeat customers will be your real test. Send press releases to contemporary culture, ethnic, food & drink, regional, travel and women's magazines.

Qualifications needed: None.

Educating yourself: Get as much practice as you can. Ask other people (not friends!) for their honest opinions, as the quality of the food items you make will be your greatest asset in this business.

Number of employees needed to start business (apart from yourself): 0

Things to watch out for: Trends in the food industry (e.g., the growing popularity of low fat foods). Make sure your food preparation and packaging processes are hygienic. Choose food items that are most likely to withstand a delivery by mail.

Additional income: You can expand into home brewery. Keep in mind, however, that this involves a much larger investment as well as licensing.

Find a similar business at:
http://www.IllinoisAmishCountry.com/WLPantry/gifthome.htm

37. SIGNS

Since this is supposed to be an online business with a nationwide appeal, large signs that require installation are of course out of the question. No one will order an awning or a large metal storefront sign from an online vendor. However, every store needs small, sometimes temporary signs: price lists, special sale signs, notes to patrons, etcetera. These are relatively small, inexpensive paper signs, and ordering them from an online business may prove more convenient and cost effective than handing the job over to a local sign maker.

A well designed Web site will take care of the ordering process for you. The customer will choose the size and color of the sign, and use special forms to key in the sign's content and give instructions for font size, layout and graphic design. A deposit will then be taken from the customer, and a layout of the sign will be sent to him for approval (via e-mail attachments, fax, or land mail) before the actual work begins. Another option your site should give customers is the ability to transfer to you the layout of the sign as they prepared it on their own word processor.

Start-up investment (other than Internet site costs and connection fees): $10,000-$100,000. If you choose to stick to paper signs only, your start up cost will be low. Any upgrading (e.g., to plastic signs) would involve the purchase of expensive machinery.

International potential: Yes.

Special promotional strategies (in addition to those discussed in chapter 5): Send press releases to trade journals and magazines that are likely to be read by small business owners. Establish links in sites that offer services for businesses.

Qualifications needed: None.

Educating yourself: Visit several stores and learn what kinds of signs are being used by them (material, layout). Practice until you are able to come up with a high quality product.

Number of employees needed to start business (apart from yourself): 0

Things to watch out for: High competition. Investing in machinery for signs that will not sell on the Internet (e.g., large metal signs).

Additional income: Sell small, custom made neon signs that do not require installation. You will need some training, but this is a very profitable business.

Find a similar business at:
http://www.netcomuk.co.uk/~pukka/signs.html#3

38. LABELS AND STICKERS

This is a relatively easy business whose products are always in demand. Almost every business needs self-adhesive labels for a variety of reasons — marking products, marking quality control checks, advertising, giving them away to customers, etcetera. Labels and stickers are purchased more often than signs, and are easier to sell over the Internet.

You have to invest in printing machinery, at least for basic types of labels. Your site should be simple and user friendly. The customer will choose one label design and size, and key in the text, together with any special instructions. The finished layout will then be sent to the customer for approval, and once you receive it, you can move on to the conventional side of the business — printing and shipping.

Start-up investment (other than Internet site costs and connection fees): $15,000-$100,000

International potential: None.

Special promotional strategies (in addition to those discussed in chapter 5): This type of business relies on repeat costumers. Make sure you offer good deals and high quality output. Businesses that switch from their current supplier to a new one usually do so because of quality problems (faded ink, poor alignment) as well as economic reasons. Send free samples of your previous work to any visitor to your site who requests it. Press releases will not enthral editors unless your site offers additional, unique services or features. You may want to try direct mail (not e-mail!) during your first months in business.

Qualifications needed: None.

Educating yourself: Aside from learning to operate your machinery, all you need do is study the market: price structures, acceptable delivery time, special services for customers.

Number of employees needed to start business (apart from yourself): 0

Things to watch out for: Don't invest too heavily in machinery during the initial stage. Until you are sure of a solid customer base, a used machine for printing basic labels will do.

Additional income: Bumper stickers. This is a business in its own right. Your site can allow customers to select from several dozens of "smart-alecky" stickers, or design their own. This option is particularly good if you don't want to invest too much in machinery.

Find a similar business at: http://www.aeda.com/fastlabels/

39. ONLINE WEIGHT CONTROL SERVICE

Unlike conventional weight loss centers, which offer on-premises services such as aerobic dances, sliding scales and motivational speakers, an online weight control service can deal only with consultation and retail. You can offer the following services in your site:

1. Free information: nutritional charts, information about diets and exercise, recipes, expert advice, FAQs, diet horror stories. Cover all weight control and related subjects as thoroughly as the space in your site will allow. This will turn your site into a high-traffic free center, and, with statistics classifying about 50 percent of the American population as overweight, you should have absolutely no problem finding visitors.

2. One-on-one consultation. For example: the customers will key-in their personal data, such as weight, age, type of occupation, sex. You will create a personalized program for them based upon this data and send it right to their e-mail box. You can also set an automated feature that will use the customer's data to calculate and display a more limited output: the number of calories this customer should consume every day, for instance.

3. Selling related products: appetite suppressant foods, motivational

video and audio cassettes, books.

Start-up investment (other than Internet site costs and connection fees): $1,000-$5,000

International potential: Yes.

Special promotional strategies (in addition to those discussed in chapter 5): If you offer a large base of free information in your site, word of mouth will probably take care of promotion for you, and press releases will stand a good chance of being published. Monitor relevant newsgroups.

Qualifications needed: If you intend to offer professional consultation services, a license is required in some states.

Educating yourself: Courses, seminars, books, university education.

Number of employees needed to start business (apart from yourself): 0

Things to watch out for: If you intend to offer consultation services you must get liability insurance.

Additional income: Selling exercise equipment. You can work on a drop-ship basis with one of the exercise equipment manufacturers and save yourself the cost of keeping an inventory.

Find a similar business at:
http://www.telepath.com/medcheck/diet.html

40. ONLINE TROUBLESHOOTING SERVICE

For every piece of equipment that has to be sent out to the shop for repair, dozens of other malfunctioning appliances simply require the pressing of the right button. Computers are especially sensitive to user errors — most computer owners are panic stricken whenever, due to the altering of a few lines in their config file, they find themselves with an inoperable machine that denies them access to their own files.

For your Internet site, choose the type of equipment of which you have a fair understanding and experience. Computers are probably going to be your best choice because most Internet users own a PC, and because this is the household machine people have the most difficulties with. Naturally, you can add several other items — VCRs, CD players, even basic auto problems.

The best approach for this business will be to make your troubleshooting lists free for public viewing. Making your site a free center for owners of malfunctioning devices will help you to generate income through the following services:

1. One on one consultation. Through chat programs or e-mail you can work out the problem with the customer in real time. Charge by the hour, by the message or by assignment.

2. Sell information packages. For example, lists of FAQs pertaining to a specific type of appliances and how to fix them.

3. Sell owner's manuals, technical guides, courses, and books. A large list of such items displayed in your site may by itself be a good reason for people to visit it.

4. Accept advertising.

Start-up investment (other than Internet site costs and connection fees): $1,000-$5,000

International potential: Yes.

Special promotional strategies (in addition to those discussed in

chapter 5): Press releases emphasizing the free services that your site offers may interest editors of technical, computer, or consumer magazines. Establish links in online electronics or appliance stores.

Qualifications needed: None. However, a technical or computer background is a definite plus.

Educating yourself: You will have to learn as much as you can about the equipment you choose to service. Get every possible manual and relevant technical literature, and practice.

Number of employees needed to start business (apart from yourself): 0

Things to watch out for: Your fees cannot be set high, or people will prefer to deal with a repair shop.

Additional income: You can sell parts and accessories. For example, if you have isolated a customer's problem and found out that its source is insufficient memory (in his PC), you can sell him the required memory chips.

Find a similar business at:
http://www.daileyint.com/hmdpc/handtoc.htm

41. SOFTWARE

Any business that deals with PCs and related services will make a good Internet business, and selling software is probably one of the best businesses in this category. A software vendor benefits from the Internet in another way — software can be downloaded instantly from your site to the customer's computer, no land delivery needed. Of course, particularly long software should better be sent by mail due to long downloading time. You can offer the following types of services and products in your site:

1. Allowing customers to download software for a fee. You either have to create your own software (e.g., a comprehensive list of names and addresses of all U.S. residents) or pay royalties to the creator.

2. Selling software that cannot be downloaded — titles you could not obtain permission from the creator to transfer via the Internet. Most of the software you will find in a conventional software store fall into this category, and you will have to sell them as you would any other product — as-is and in their original sealed packages.

3. Shareware software. This is the cash-upon-approval approach. The customer downloads the software, which is free for a 30 to 90 days trial period. Unless the customer pays for the software at the end of this period, the software will expire and will not be usable anymore. You will either have to create your own software to license as shareware, or reach an agreement with another software creator.

4. Freeware. The customer will download the software for free and use it for an unlimited time. Your reward? If you are the software's creator, it can come in several ways: selling upgrades, directing the customer to your site (if the freeware is a browser, for instance), accepting advertising, etcetera. If you are not the software's creator, you can use the free software you offer in your site only to generate traffic and increase your site's popularity to a point where you can charge for advertising. It is always a good idea to offer free software in your site, even if has only a remote connection to your business's main service or product. Many of the freeware software creators (e.g., Netscape) allow you to establish links to their sites, or in other words to include their freeware with your site's freeware selection.

Start-up investment (other than Internet site costs and connection fees): $10,000-$100,000

International potential: Yes.

Special promotional strategies (in addition to those discussed in chapter 5): Send press releases to entertainment, computer and software magazines. Monitor relevant newsgroups. Try to build your site's reputation as "one of the largest collections of freeware on the Internet."

Qualifications needed: If you want to create your own software, you must have a great deal of programming knowledge and experience.

Educating yourself: Scan the online world for businesses that create freeware and ask their permission to establish a link to their sites. Subscribe to all trade magazines and publications.

Number of employees needed to start business (apart from yourself): 0

Things to watch out for: This is a rapidly changing business. If you decide to keep an inventory, make sure you do not wind up with dead items. Creating new software is a very hard and costly process, and unless you know a lot about both programming and market trends, stick to selling other creators' products.

Additional income: Selling computer and software books.

Find a similar business at: http://www.hotfiles.com

42. ONLINE CLASSIFIED ADS

This type of business exists entirely online. There is no inventory, no delivery, no personal contact with customers. The site, much like a newspaper's classified section, will be divided according to categories: cars for sale, home appliances, help wanted, business opportunities and so on. The customers will write their own messages according to the number of words they paid for. However, unlike a newspaper, which requires advertisers to stick to a fixed deadline that is set at least two to three days prior to publication, an online classified ads site can place ads instantaneously.

Another option open for you is to accept classified ads for free. Your income, of course, will derive from (commercial) advertising fees or from charging customers a percentage of the advertised price only upon successful selling of the item. The ad will continue to run until the item is sold, so in the event the customer decides to be less than honest about the sale, they will continue to be bothered by phone calls or e-mail messages for a very long time.

This site can easily be made fully automated, and will probably require less than an hour a week for operating. The site will not require constant updating. Being so undemanding, this is an ideal business for people who decide to keep their full time day job.

Start-up investment (other than Internet site costs and connection fees): $1,000-$5,000

International potential: Yes

Special promotional strategies (in addition to those discussed in chapter 5): Start out with free advertising. When the site becomes large enough, start charging fees gradually. For example, start charging only from the second week an ad is running. Monitor newsgroups. Make sure the key words you use for your search engine listings will include: buying, selling, classified, for sale, cars, help wanted, business, ads, etcetera. Send press releases to magazines that deal with the auto industry, home furnishing, real estate and every other category you plan to include in your classified ads.

Qualifications needed: None.

Number of employees needed to start business (apart from yourself): 0

Things to watch out for: Reserve the right to alter or altogether cancel a classified ad that uses profanity or graphic language, so that your site will not lose potential customers who may be offended.

Additional income: Over time, you can compile and sell phone number lists to direct marketing companies. For example, people who sell their house are about to move and will therefore interest real estate agencies, insurance companies, movers, interior decorators, carpet merchants and such.

Find a similar business at:
http://www.commercial.net/vault/ads/

43. RARE/ANTIQUE PARTS SEARCHER

Any collector of antiques, be it cars, aircrafts, appliances or other, must have experienced this problem at least several times in his life: how to find a part for something that has been out of production for half a century or more? Producing rare parts, especially for cars, has become an industry in its own right. Some businesses specialize in buying original parts (e.g., from junk yards or collectors) and stocking them. Others manufacture replacement parts, which are of a lesser value in the market, but are still greatly in demand.

To succeed in this business, you must specialize in one or more areas (e.g., body parts for Ford model T). Your job is to bring the collector, who is in need of a certain part, together with the vendor or another collector who has it. If no such original part is found, or if the price is too high, you can help the customer find a replacement part.

You can set your fees either by the hour or per item. You can become a broker — the customer places a deposit, and you buy the part for him. Most of your job will be done through e-mail or telephone calls. Your site can be simple, even one page long, but you should consider offering some free information or services for collectors to attract visitors.

Start-up investment (other than Internet site costs and connection fees): $1,000-$5,000

International potential: Yes. However, some countries limit or altogether ban the removal of certain antiques beyond their borders.

Special promotional strategies (in addition to those discussed in chapter 5): Send press releases to collector magazines. Place ads in collector magazines. Link to and from similar sites.

Qualifications needed: None.

Educating yourself: Once you have chosen the type of antiques or rare items you are going to specialize in, subscribe to every possible publication on the subject, and buy every relevant reference book. Compile a list of all used, antique and hard-to-get parts dealers, as well as manufacturers of replacement and rebuilt parts. The more information you have at your fingertips, the faster it will take you to locate a part.

Number of employees needed to start business (apart from yourself): 0

Things to watch out for: Your success depends largely on the speed of your search. If a collector is looking for a radiator for a '57 Chevy Belair, for instance, he is likely to contact several dealers in addition to your business. You will have to be able to beat them to it or you will find that your customer has already found the part by the time you contact him again. It will take you some time to build your reputation to a point where collectors will leave a deposit with you and trust you alone with the search job.

Additional income: Selling catalogs and literature about repairs, maintenance and other relevant collectors' information. A referral service for repair and restoration shops.

Find a similar business at: http://www.rareparts.com

44. HOME SCHOOLING CONSULTATION SERVICE

Home schooling has many disadvantages, chief among them the implications it might have on a child's social abilities. However, in some cases, the parents, who cannot afford private schooling, feel that public schools (especially in violent neighborhoods) are not safe and subject the child to bad influences. Others prefer home schooling for religious reasons. Your job is to help the parents educate their children.

You can:

1. Offer one on one consultation through e-mail or chat programs/ Internet telephony. This approach deals with problems as they arise and helps the parents in their day to day teaching effort.

2. Set up a curriculum that will fit the needs of the students and meet the educational standards set by the state.

3. Sell or recommend textbooks, teachers' editions and other learning aids.

4. Refer the students to other educational activities, such as special (local) seminars and classes, and recommend visits to places of educational value such as museums or historic sites.

In addition, dedicate as many pages as you can in your site to free information. Parents who have decided to walk this path need all the help they can get.

Start-up investment (other than Internet site costs and connection fees): $1,000-$10,000

International potential: You can help families who have to spend a long time abroad and do not want to neglect their children's education.

Special promotional strategies (in addition to those discussed in chapter 5): Send press releases to education and counseling magazines. Monitor relevant newsgroups.

Qualifications needed: Teaching certificate.

Educating yourself: Study for a degree in education.

Number of employees needed to start business (apart from yourself): 0

Things to watch out for: Running this business is a great responsibility. Parents will be trusting you with their children's education. Unlike many other businesses, this one cannot go together with a learn-as-you-earn approach.

Additional income: Offer adult education courses.

Find a similar business at: http://www.midnightbeach.com/hs

45. FOREIGN COMPANIES' REPRESENTATIVE

The Internet allows businesses to communicate with one another across border lines and continents without incurring the expense of long distance charges. International transactions are thus made easier and faster, and communication channels are made more open. However, many limitations will always hinder any international transaction — customs regulations, standards, documentation, licensing, contact with local authorities. These things cannot be dealt with from abroad. Any company wishing to do more than occasional business in a different country must therefore be able to establish an office there. Such an office involves a large investment (typically no less than $100,000 a year) which has to be spent on staff, office rental, office supplies and similar expenses.

For a small business that does not need a full time representation in foreign countries and that does not expect to do enough business to cover such high expenses, setting up this kind of an office is a not a good idea.

This is where you come in. Taking your orders through the Internet, you can represent a small to medium foreign company in the U.S., and perform, among others, the following services for them:

1. Handling all correspondence with local corporations and government agencies.

2. Handling promotion and advertising. Writing and sending press releases to U.S. magazines.

3. Finding and employing the services of any local business that may be required by your customers (e.g., translators, delivery trucks, warehouses, CPAs, Lawyers).

4. Opening a local subsidiary or a U.S. corporation under which the company you represent will conduct business in the U.S.

5. Providing a local center that will accept telephone calls and mail on behalf of the foreign company, and which will transfer their contents to them by e-mail.

6. Offering a consultation service for a variety of business issues — import regulations, dealing with U.S. banks, local advertising, exhibitions and trade shows, etcetera.

Your fees will depend not only on the amount of work you will have to put into representing your customer, but also on the extent of business initiative on your part. If the services you provide for your customer are mostly technical (finding a warehouse, dealing with import and export) you will probably not charge as much as you would a customer for whom you have actively searched for clients, established new business contacts and dealt with promotion.

Start-up investment (other than Internet site costs and connection fees): $1,000-$5,000

International potential: Yes.

Special promotional strategies (in addition to those discussed in chapter 5): Issue press releases to foreign business and trade magazines. Send direct land mail to potential customers. Networking (e.g., attending trade shows).

Qualifications needed: Some experience in conducting international business.

Educating yourself: Of the business areas you have to master, import regulations is paramount. It is also important to study international money transactions (procedures and schedules). Compile a list of distributors and jobbers for the products you are about to represent.

Number of employees needed to start business (apart from yourself): 0

Things to watch out for: You will have to work closely with a lawyer and a CPA. Some foreign companies have unrealistic expectations about raising funds in the U.S. while their actual prospects are dim because they are not monitored by U.S. credit bureaus.

Additional income: Performing some of the services you arrange for your customer yourself— accounting, distributing, promotion.

Find a similar business at: http://www.gvgroup.com

46. E-MAIL RESPONDER

Yes, mailbots can do that, too. However, mailbots do not have a personal touch. At best they can be programmed to select the message they send out according to the key words they receive; and so the customer must phrase his message to suit the mailbot, often limiting it to just one word. But what happens if the customer wants to write a full message, or to phrase a question that would express his own concerns or particular problems? For example, let us assume that a national pet-shop chain sets up an online presence to help promote its conventional stores. An auto responder may give customers the address of the store closest to them, and maybe some general details, but that is all. If a customer sends an e-mail message that reads "Does your Kansas City location carry rainbow boas?" no auto responder will be able to help him, simple as this question may be. Hiring a special Webmaster to take care of this problem is usually not a good economic decision for most small companies.

Your business will send a personalized response to e-mail inquiries. You will receive all the e-mail messages sent to your clients, and your clients will supply you with the material needed to answer most questions (in the above example — inventories, opening hours, basic product information). You can work with several online businesses at the same time, and your job will consist mainly of sitting in front of the computer answering e-mail messages all day. In some instances you will need, of course, to contact your client and ask for more information. In a sense, you will become a part time customer service representative.

Start-up investment (other than Internet site costs and connection fees): $1,000-$5,000

International potential: Yes.

Special promotional strategies (in addition to those discussed in chapter 5): Send press releases to business, trade and online magazines. Establish links in sites that offer services for businesses. Contact server services and offer them a commission or a flat fee for recommending you to their customers (especially those who had set up their sites recently, or who had set up mailbots).

Qualifications needed: None.

Educating yourself: Ask the businesses you work for what questions their customers typically ask, and compile a FAQ list.

Number of employees needed to start business (apart from yourself): 0

Things to watch out for: Don't charge a flat monthly fee unless you are certain that you can accurately estimate the number of incoming e-mail messages your client is going to receive. Make sure you take down every reply your customer has instructed you to give — they would not like it if you call them twice a day with the same question.

Additional income: Offer your customers a complete package of Web site maintenance — updating, graphic design, etc.

Find a similar business at:http://empower.cyberplex.com/ (this company deals with Web based solutions to e-mail inquiries)

47. ONLINE MALL

As discussed in page 43, there are two kinds of online malls: those which operate as the vendors' only outlet to the online world, and those that offer only listings and links to the vendors' sites. Operating the first type of online mall is a very costly, complicated matter that in essence is not much different from operating a small server service (with the difference that the number of businesses belonging to the same category may be limited in a mall).

To set up an online mall of any kind is to anticipate tremendously high online traffic. You will probably want a dedicated connection to the Internet for your business (see page 40), which is very expensive. You may also have to employ (as subcontractors, at least) Web site creators and consultants that will help your customers set up their virtual shops. If all you provide are just links to the vendors' Internet sites your job is simpler, of course, but you will still have to maintain a user friendly menu and a graphically appealing site that will encourage visitors to come back, and you will still have to handle a lot of traffic.

The main service that vendors will come to expect of you is promotion. In addition to on-site promotion (free info, free software and other crowd-pulling gimmicks) you will have to invest heavily in every other possible means of promotion and, within reason, advertising.

Start-up investment (other than Internet site costs and connection fees): $20,000-$100,000

International potential: Yes.

Special promotional strategies (in addition to those discussed in chapter 5): Send press releases to almost all kinds of magazines. Contact vendors directly and offer special introductory deals (e.g., free Web page creating). You will spend most of your time promoting your vendors' businesses, and will also have to advertise, especially online (e.g., What's-New listings). Give your mall an original angle, a unique form or a new free service that will help you lure in customers.

Qualifications needed: None.

Educating yourself: Studying similar online malls and learning where you can find the right niche for yourself.

Number of employees needed to start business (apart from yourself): 0-2

Things to watch out for: The first customers are the hardest to get. You may want to start with a free three months listing (or longer) in order to build up your mall. If you are not sure of success, you can decrease your investment by setting up your business with a server service at first. However, as soon as business picks up and the number of hits begins to grow, you will have to invest in a dedicated connection or many users will not be able to reach your site during peak hours.

Additional income: Accepting advertising (on your home page, main menu) is a must for a high traffic site such as this. You can offer a variety of services to the vendors in your mall — from consultation to Web site designing.

Find a similar business at: http://mall4all.com/mall.htm

48. ONLINE PROMOTER

Since dealing with promotion is going to take up so much of your time anyway, why not turn it into a business in its own right? Much like an advertising agency, you will find the best advertising spots both online and off-line for your clients. However — your main business will be promotion consultation rather than ad placement. Every promotional opportunity and strategy described in chapter 5, plus those you will undoubtedly come across yourself while working with the Internet, will be made known to your clients for a fee. You can offer these services in your site:

1. Tailoring a special promotional package according to the nature and individual needs of your client's business.

2. Consultation services. Answering specific questions for your clients in matters of promotion and advertising strategies.

3. Selling lists and addresses of all search engines, directories, link centers, magazine editors and other online and off-line promotional services and opportunities.

4. Doing the promotional work for the client. Rather than sending your client the above lists, you will make all contacts with the appropriate channels of promotion for him.

Start-up investment (other than Internet site costs and connection fees): $5,000-$10,000

International potential: Yes.

Special promotional strategies (in addition to those discussed in chapter 5): You will have to over-promote this business — seeing is believing and if this is the service you sell, your potential customers will expect you to practice what you preach. A strong presence online and off-line achieved by free promotion will convince them that you know what you are talking about. However, you may also want to spend a little on effective paid promotion.

Qualifications needed: None, but previous online business experience will help.

Educating yourself: You will have to become an expert on online promotion, which means spending many hours surfing the Internet in search of new ideas and strategies.

Number of employees needed to start business (apart from yourself): 0

Things to watch out for: Finding free promotion opportunities is your main service and the reason for most clients to come to you. They will tend to be less enthusiastic about using your services if they learn that most of what you deal with is paid advertising. Invest your advertising budget in online promotion (listings in What's New services, for instance) instead of plain online ads.

Additional income: Selling information packages and books on promotion, advertising, marketing, business management.

Find a similar business at:
http://www.mmgco.com/campaign.html

49. FIREWALL/SECURITY CONSULTANT

Security systems are used with LANs (see page 23) that connect directly to the Internet. These small independent networks, consisting of several computers, need security systems to protect them from unauthorized access by Internet users, who might penetrate or alter sensitive files. In other words, these security systems (also known as firewalls) protect the internal networks from misuse by users of the external network.

This is not an easy business to start, and it requires a great deal of understanding of computers and UNIX. This is also one of the only online businesses that require you to travel to the customer's location. However, the rewards are quite high — security consultants may earn as much as $100-$200 an hour, and charge $3,000-$5,000 for an average project. Your customers are medium to large size corporations who connect directly to the Internet.

Start-up investment (other than Internet site costs and connection fees): $1,000-$5,000

International potential: None.

Special promotional strategies (in addition to those discussed in chapter 5): Issue press releases to business, trade, computer and online magazines. Establish links in sites that offer services for businesses and executives. This in one of the few Internet businesses for which a Yellow Pages listing might be a good idea, but only in major business-to-business directories.

Qualifications needed: A background in programming and UNIX.

Educating yourself: Read all available literature on firewalls and UNIX. Practice. Become an apprentice — offer to work for an established security consultation service for a few months without pay.

Number of employees needed to start business (apart from yourself): 0

Things to watch out for: Fees may go down. However, we are not likely to see anything like the drastic drop the HTML professionals have experienced. Security systems are far too complicated and require on-site installation.

Additional income: Internet programing consultation. Network design and maintenance.

Find a similar business at:
http://www.nsli.com/

50. ONLINE CHESS/BRIDGE LESSONS

People invest in special classes and literature in order to become better chess or bridge players. Whole industries — books, clubs, game supply manufacturers, teachers — are making a living out of these leisure activities. You can do the same in your site, and offer the following services:

1. One-on-one lessons, either through e-mail or special game software with an online playing option. You will have to either

find the latter as freeware or pay the creator for every customer who downloads a copy (unless the customer already owns a copy of a software you use). You will also need to use chat programs to converse with the students in real time and offer your advice and criticism.

2. Offer free tips, strategies and other relevant information in your site (major tournament results, game history).

3. Sell game boards or other related equipment and literature.

4. Become a matchmaker for online playing partners. Arrange competitions and tournaments.

Start-up investment (other than Internet site costs and connection fees): $5,000-$10,000

International potential: Yes.

Special promotional strategies (in addition to those discussed in chapter 5): Issue press releases to game, puzzle, novelty and hobby magazines. Give away prizes to the winners in your site's tournaments. Establish links in sites that deal with games, hobbies or other recreational activities.

Qualifications needed: Adequate game skills.

Educating yourself: For you, it is far more important to know how to teach a game than to be a good player. Study teaching methods for the game you have chosen as well as other games or activities.

Number of employees needed to start business (apart from yourself): 0

Things to watch out for: Building your reputation will take time, and until you are able to support yourself by game lessons alone, you will have to rely on retail to keep you going. Keep an inventory of books, game software, game boards and similar products.

Additional income: You are, of course, not limited to chess and bridge alone, and your site can be used to teach and sell equipment for many other popular games.

Find a similar business at: http://www.chessclub.com

51. ONLINE MALL REPRESENTATIVE

Unlike an online mall operator, an online mall representative's job is limited to getting as many businesses as possible to join a mall. You work on a commission basis with one of the large online malls, and in effect act as the mall's promoter or direct mail service. The main advantage of this business is the low start up cost — you don't even need to buy a computer. You can contact your prospects by phone, mail or in person.

A computer, however, may help you a lot in this business. You don't need an online presence (this is the only business in this book that does not require a site), but a simple dial-up account will allow you to contact online businesses and greatly improve your chances of finding customers.

Convincing online businesses to list themselves with an online mall isn't difficult. If the mall's fees are reasonable and it has a good reputation, many businesses will jump at the chance to gain additional online exposure.

In addition to online businesses, you should try to interest conventional businesses in joining the mall (which in this case will act also as their server service, providing them with their only online presence). Here your job is harder. Some businesses that might benefit tremendously from having an online presence, decline to establish a site because they believe it to be a complex and costly matter that requires programming skills. You will get their business by explaining to them how simple and inexpensive joining an online mall really is.

Start-up investment (other than Internet site costs and connection fees): $0-$3,000

International potential: Yes (for online businesses only).

Special promotional strategies (in addition to those discussed in chapter 5): You can find your potential customers on the Internet, in the yellow pages or by contacting the businesses in your neighborhood or town in person.

Qualifications needed: None.

Number of employees needed to start business (apart from yourself): 0

Things to watch out for: This business requires little more than your time, and this is all you stand to lose. However, if after three months you are still unable to make more than $150 a week — quit! Your time is a valuable commodity, too.

Additional income: Once you feel confident in your ability to attract vendors to an online mall, you may want to open your own. The investment required for this is of course on a totally different scale.

52. ONLINE DISTRIBUTOR

Just like a conventional distributor, your job will be to sell a product to stores and other retailers. You, however, can reach many of your customers online and know right away what kind of products they are selling as well as which products are missing from their selection. For example, let us assume that you are selling picture frames. Such an item can interest photo shops, art shops, stationery stores and general stores. If you want to locate any of the above stores that does not carry frames yet, you would have to walk the streets for many days in search of them or at least make hundreds of phone calls (which will never give you an accurate picture of the store's inventory). By visiting online businesses, however, you can find out in seconds whether or not the vendor already carries frames (or, more specifically, your line of frames). The time needed to find potential customers is decreased significantly.

Another option you can offer your customers (who are, of course, online businesses), especially if you are handling hard to move items, is drop shipment. Here's how it works: suppose the item you have for sale is decorative beer mugs. First, you locate every possible online vendor through which such an item can be sold (even seemingly unrelated businesses such as stationery, gifts, art, sport). Next, approach them and ask to establish a link (which will include your product's description and picture) to your site. The vendor will receive a percentage of the sale (20-40%) and you will take care of the shipping and handling, and the payment processing. Few online vendors will reject such an offer, which requires them only to establish a link in their site and leave the rest to you. As for your products — even slow moving items will sell if they are displayed on hundreds of different online locations.

Start-up investment (other than Internet site costs and connection fees): $10,000 +

International potential: Yes.

Special promotional strategies (in addition to those discussed in chapter 5): Send press releases (if you come out with a new product) to trade magazines. Promoting this business involves direct contact with potential customers (businesses).

Qualifications needed: None.

Educating yourself: Find the right, marketable product.

Number of employees needed to start business (apart from yourself): 0

Things to watch out for: Investing too heavily in an item that cannot be moved. Buying huge quantities of a dead item just because it was offered at a very low price.

Additional income: Start an online price club.

Find a similar business at:
http://www.intelligent.com.au/IT/index.asp

53. REFERRAL SERVICE

Unlike the Yellow Pages, this online service will not list *everyone*. You need to work with the Better Business Bureau and rely on their records as well as customers' comments in order to seek out the reputable businesses you can honestly recommend to your customers. Who will use your services? Someone who is looking for a lawyer, for example, and has no idea which of the hundreds of lawyers listed in the Yellow Pages he should turn to. People who are looking for a good dentist, plumber, or other professional will come to you. Your customers will include people who need to use a certain practitioner for the first time, who are displeased with their current service, or who have just moved to a new city.

You can charge visitors to your site for access to your list of rated professionals, of course, but this will greatly limit your site's popularity. The best approach is to make these lists available to anyone free of charge, and then charge a referral fee from the business you have sent a customer to. If the fee is reasonable, many businesses will be happy to work with you. After all, we all need advertising, and *this* form of advertising only needs to be paid for when it actually works.

Start-up investment (other than Internet site costs and connection fees): $1,000-$5,000

International potential: None.

Special promotional strategies (in addition to those discussed in chapter 5): Register your business with all the search engines under key words such as: lawyer, plumber, dentist, electrician, summer camp, air conditioning repair, etcetera. This way, Internet users will find you whenever they are looking for any one of the above professionals.

Qualifications needed: None.

Educating yourself: Search all consumer and government publications for information about professional people, practices and businesses. Contact the Better Business Bureau.

Number of employees needed to start business (apart from yourself): 0

Things to watch out for: Collecting your referral fees from the businesses you recommend and keeping track of the right amount due is not always easy. There will always be ways to trick referral services. However, over time you will learn who among the businesses you list is honest and who should be dropped from the list.

Additional income: Recommend restaurants, hotels, travel agents. Accept advertising (this is a potentially high traffic site).

Find a similar business at: http://www.campfinders.com/

54. SENIOR CITIZENS' INTERNET CENTER

The number of senior citizens with Internet access is growing rapidly. This is a perfect pastime for people with lots of time on their hands. Many of them, however, especially those who are not computer literate (the vast majority), feel overwhelmed by the seemingly complex online world. They need help in understanding basic Internet and computer terms, and in comprehending and exploring the full spectrum of the Internet.

Your site should be designed in such a way that your senior citizen customers will want to set it as the first page in their browser (i.e. it will be visited automatically whenever the user connects to the Internet). It has to be excessively user friendly, and equipped with hundreds of useful links. The fonts have to be larger than average and the pages should not overwhelm the user with long, condensed texts. Display the following features on your site:

1. Basic Internet information and terminology.

2. Links. Help your visitors reach important or popular Internet sites by displaying clear, descriptive information about the linked sites and their content.

3. Troubleshooting lists (computer and online problems) in plain English.

4. Consultation through chat programs (especially vocal).

5. A virtual store for special devices and items for senior citizens (you are not limited to computer equipment, of course) and Internet courses (books or software).

Your income will be derived from the fourth and fifth categories as well as from accepting advertising.

As health care and medical services improve, the percentage of people over 65 in the general population is constantly on the rise. In addition, old people today tend to be wealthier than ever before. The demand for businesses that cater to the elderly, therefore, is headed only one way — up.

Start-up investment (other than Internet site costs and connection fees): $5,000-$25,000

International potential: Yes.

Special promotional strategies (in addition to those discussed in chapter 5): Send direct land mail to senior citizen organizations and homes, and to community centers. Issue press releases to game and puzzle, health, home and garden, and retirement magazines. Establish links in similar sites (e.g., health and fitness).

Qualifications needed: None.

Educating yourself: You may want to interview a few elderly people to find out what are the main problems and difficulties they experience with the Internet. Devise ways to get around these problems.

Number of employees needed to start business (apart from yourself): 0

Things to watch out for: You may need to set up a special telephone line to better serve people who have difficulties operating their computers, and who may want to call you on the phone.

Additional income: Selling health books. Starting a senior citizens' online magazine.

Find a similar business at: http://www.senior.com/

55. ONLINE INTERPRETER

Unlike the translation of documents, interpreting is done in real time, utilizing chat programs/Internet telephony. The process is simple: one party calls you and you direct him and the other party to the chat program you are using (whether audio or text based). There, as in a three-party telephone conversation, both sides can relate ideas and information to each other through your interpreting service, and with no telecommunication costs. If you want the conversation to be more private you can (using two modems) connect to both parties and start two parallel one-on-one Internet telephony conversations. Programs such as Freetel (http://www.freetel.inter.net) allow you to do this at no cost.

This business is very simple to operate, and requires only a basic, one or two pages long, site. The Internet's fast global expansion creates a growing need for such a service among business people who must transcend the language barrier in order to promote and manage their business.

Start-up investment (other than Internet site costs and connection fees): $1,000-$5,000

International potential: Yes.

Special promotional strategies (in addition to those discussed in chapter 5): Establish links in sites that offer services for businesses. Send press releases to U.S. and foreign business and trade magazines.

Qualifications needed: Mastery of the language you intend to interpret. A certificate may be required by certain customers.

Educating yourself: Courses and literature. Search the Internet and visit business libraries of foreign consulates to find foreign businesses that are interested in doing business with U.S. companies.

Number of employees needed to start business (apart from yourself): 0

Things to watch out for: A proficiency in the language you interpret may not be enough. You may need to learn technical, medical or legal terms in order to be of use to a corporation seeking international trade and business connections.

Additional income: Translation service. Business representation.

Find a similar business at:
http://world.std.com/~ric/fridman.html (no online services).

56. ONLINE MAGAZINE

Online magazines (a.k.a. zines) are in many ways similar to their paper-based counterparts. They can revolve around one specific subject, or deal with a wide range of interests. Some online magazines are extensions of paper-based publications or media entities (e.g., New York Times, NBC), who found that an online presence for their publications is a good way to increase their viewer/reader base without undermining their main off-line businesses. For you as an operator, an online magazine has several advantages over paper based magazines:

1. No printing costs.

2. No distribution channels to work with, and no shipping and handling.

3. An online magazine can boast features that paper based magazines could never hope to offer: audio files, video files, links, direct e-mail responses.

4. International appeal. Your magazine can just as easily be read by someone in China as by your own neighbor.

Your income will be derived either from selling subscriptions, which is not recommended (not even well known magazines dare do that), or from accepting advertising and from subsequent business ventures (once you are recognized as an expert in your field, you might receive offers to give lectures, and even be called to appear as an expert witness).

Start-up investment (other than Internet site costs and connection fees): $1,000-$5,000

International potential: Yes.

Special promotional strategies (in addition to those discussed in chapter 5): Link to and from sites that deal with the same subjects as your magazine. Submit your site's URL to What's-New lists.

Qualifications needed: A thorough knowledge of the subject matter of your intended magazine, be it general business news or dirt bikes.

Educating yourself: The subject you choose for your magazine must interest enough people to justify your investment (at least in time). Spend time on research before you make a decision in this matter.

Number of employees needed to start business (apart from yourself): 0. However, you may want to rely on freelance writers for at least some of the material in your online magazine.

Things to watch out for: This is a very demanding business in terms of time and work invested. You will have to prepare a new issue either every month, or, for some publications, even every week. If your magazine becomes static and repetitious, subscribers will stop coming back in a matter of weeks.

Additional income: Consultation service (for your magazine's subject matter).

Find a similar business at: http://www.globes.co.il

57. PET CENTER

Pets, as you probably know, are big business. The businesses who make a living out of people's need of being in constant touch with the animal world include pet shops, veterinarian services, breeders, manufacturers of equipment and accessories (especially for fish tanks and bird cages), pet psychologists, grooming services, and even pet taxis.

An online pet center can include:

1 Free information. Everything pet owners should know about their dogs, cats, reptiles, rodents, piglets, tropical fish or birds should be arranged under a user friendly menu. Include statistics, new products' press releases, articles written by veterinarians or other pet experts, and FAQs.

2. Virtual pet supplies shop.

3. Consultation services.

4. Dog training courses. These can be sold in the form of books, leaflets, or through e-mail.

5. Stolen/missing pet notices. Customers post a description of their missing pet (with or without a picture), their phone number and a reward amount.

6. Referral service. Recommend veterinarians, grooming services, obedience schools, and charge those businesses a fee for every customer who has found them through your site.

Start-up investment (other than Internet site costs and connection fees): $30,000-$100,000

International potential: Yes (but selling pet supplies overseas will be limited due to shipping costs).

Special promotional strategies (in addition to those discussed in chapter 5): Issue press releases to general interests and pet magazines. Send direct land mail to associations of pet owners.

Qualifications needed: None. However, previous experience in the pet business is a definite plus.

Educating yourself: Books, publications, magazines.

Number of employees needed to start business (apart from yourself): 0

Things to watch out for: A large inventory will be required for your virtual shop. It is necessary since there are many different types of products in this business.

Additional income: An online pet magazine.

Find a similar business at: http://www.thepetchannel.com/

58. VEHICLE REPORTS ARCHIVES

Before people spend money on a motorcycle, car, or boat, they often want to learn as much as they can about the model they are about to buy. Magazines publish reports on new models at or about the time they appear on the market, but rarely afterwards. If the vehicle you want to buy is used, your chances of finding a report on it (such as a test drive) in current magazine issues are remote.

Vehicle reports archives do the search for the customers, and present them with every article (discussing the desired model) that was published in all relevant magazines since that model first rolled off the assembly line. Typically, you will have to get the magazine publishers' permission and pay royalties for every article you submit to your customer. Your main job will be to copy or scan into your computer various articles and reports, and arrange them according to model names and years. Through the Internet, you will then be able (unless your customer prefers land mail delivery) to send the articles via e-mail. Another option is to put all the articles on your site and allow users (for a fee) to select one menu item — the vehicle model they have chosen — for viewing.

Start-up investment (other than Internet site costs and connection fees): $1,000-$5,000

International potential: Yes.

Special promotional strategies (in addition to those discussed in chapter 5): Links to and from sites that deal with the automotive industry, boating, biking, loans, students' and young people's interests. Send press releases to auto, motorcycle and boat magazines. Monitor relevant newsgroups.

Qualifications needed: None.

Educating yourself: Contact every popular vehicle magazine and purchase all the old issues you can get.

Number of employees needed to start business (apart from yourself): 0

Things to watch out for: Although most will, some magazines may not give you permission to use their material.

Additional income: Consultation and referral services. Selling owner's manuals for old models.

Find a similar business at: http://www.motorcycle.com

59. TEXT-TO-PHONE SERVICE

This unique service, which can be started only on the Internet, will allow people with hearing disabilities or those who are speech impaired to participate in or initiate regular phone conversations. Let us suppose, for example, that a person with severe hearing disabilities wants to order a pizza. Unless his local pizza place is connected to the Internet, this person would have to rely on friends or relatives to make this call for him. He will experience the same problem whenever he wants to reserve a hotel room, rent a car, order items from a catalog, call friends, call to find out information or to complain, and basically whenever he wants to come in contact with the outside world.

Your business will allow this person and others like him to lead a normal, independent life. The disabled person will use a text based chat or online telephony software to convey his messages to you. You will relate this message to the third party through the telephone and key in their response, which your customer will see in text form.

When your customer is located outside your calling area, there is a good chance that the parties he will ask you to call for him involve long distance, even international dialing. You can get around this problem in several ways:

1. Charge your customer for the telephone call.

2. Work with local agents. These will be people who reside in the same area code as your customer. You will contact them through the Internet, and they will work with you for a fee. These local agents can be students whom you will recruit as sub contractors through the Internet, for example.

3. If your customer has speakers/mic in his computer and a separate line for the modem, you can use his computer to talk to the third party through his telephone. A simple device or software will do this even more effectively, and is worth the investment if the customer plans to use your services often.

4. Use conference calls (your customer will call both you and the third party).

5. Use special features long distance companies offer. For example, a calling card number that allows you to make a call from one telephone line and charge it to another account (your customer's).

Start-up investment (other than Internet site costs and connection fees): $1,000-$5,000

International potential: Yes.

Special promotional strategies (in addition to those discussed in chapter 5): Send press releases to disabilities, health, regional and retirement magazines. Contact organizations for people with hearing/speech disabilities. Contact retirement homes and senior citizens organizations.

Qualifications needed: None.

Number of employees needed to start business (apart from yourself): 0

Things to watch out for: Convincing the third parties you are calling to be patient with you (and your customer) and wait for you to transfer messages from text to vocal and vice versa.

Additional income: You can offer an opposite service — people without an Internet access will call you on the telephone in order to leave a message in someone's e-mail box.

60. IMMIGRATION CONSULTANT

With immigration at its highest rate since the turn of the century and immigration laws as complex as they have ever been, the demand for immigration and naturalization consultants grows steadily. An immigration consultant helps clients in dealing with the INS (Immigration and Naturalization Service) home and abroad. In addition to helping them obtain permanent resident's status (green card), you will supply your clients with the right forms, help them extend their tourist or work visas, deal with deportations and perform other important services for them.

Your site should offer visitors the following options:

1. One on one consultation through e-mail or chat programs.

2. Free information and FAQs about a variety of subjects, from deportation to citizenship.

3. Special information packages and advice (free or otherwise) for foreign residents who are interested in immigrating to the U.S.A., in obtaining a working visa, or who are simply having trouble getting the basic B-1/B-2 tourist visas. As so many foreign residents experience difficulties in this area — even in obtaining simple tourist visas — this service can dramatically increase the popularity of your site.

4. A visitors' contributions section, where visitors to your site can share their past experiences with the immigration authorities (including horror-stories) with other visitors.

5. A referral service (for immigration lawyers, translators).

Start-up investment (other than Internet site costs and connection fees): $1,000-$5,000

International potential: Yes.

Special promotional strategies (in addition to those discussed in chapter 5): Establish links in foreign travel agencies and sites that are of interest to foreign visitors.

Qualifications needed: A thorough knowledge of immigration laws and procedures. A license may be required in some cases.

Educating yourself: Simple matters such as extending the validity of a tourist visa can be learned in minutes just by calling the INS. For more complex services, learn from books, publications, courses, university education, and consultation. Find out what are the most common problems that tourists seeking visas to the U.S.A. have to tackle.

Number of employees needed to start business (apart from yourself): 0

Things to watch out for: Some practices are considered illegal and may lead to fines or even jail sentences. For example, obtaining false statements regarding a person's supposed employment by a sponsor. Dealing with permanent residence visas is a complex matter that requires at least some experience.

Additional income: Tourist information and services.

Find a similar business at: http://ilw.com

61. FAMILY PROBLEMS CENTER

Families are exposed to more than their fair share of problems: stress, children's problems, teenagers' problems, depressions, anxieties, addiction, relationship problems, guilt, divorce. With so many issues to worry about, it is no wonder that many families find themselves in need of guidance from time to time. In your site, they will find:

1. Articles (written by psychologists or counselors) and information about the various subjects mentioned above.

2. FAQ files.

3. A consultation service (if you hold a degree in psychology and a license), which can be offered either as one on one (through e-mail) or through discussion or therapy groups (using chat programs) that you will form.

4. A virtual shop for related books, publications, video and audio cassettes. If you cannot offer consultation services, this will be your main source of income.

5. A referral service. Your income will derive from referral fees paid by special counselors and other professionals for every customer you send them.

Start-up investment (other than Internet site costs and connection fees): $1,000-$30,000

International potential: Limited to countries with whose culture, society structure, and unique problems you are well acquainted.

Special promotional strategies (in addition to those discussed in chapter 5): Send press releases to general interests, entertainment, women's magazines. Monitor relevant newsgroups.

Qualifications needed: If you intend to offer counseling services on your site, you will need a degree in psychology and a license.

Educating yourself: Read all related publications and ask contributors for permission to post their articles to your site.

Number of employees needed to start business (apart from yourself): 0

Things to watch out for: The articles displayed in this site must be changed constantly in order to ensure visitors' return. Don't expect visitors to use your services or buy your products during their first visit. You have to contact the authorities whenever you believe that you are dealing with a case of physical abuse.

Additional income: Selling divorce information packages or kits and offering a referral service for divorce lawyers.

Find a similar business at: http://www.agony.org/Homepage.html

62. BUSINESS AND LEGAL FORMS

Every business needs forms. Forms are used both for daily business transactions (invoices, packing slips, receipts) as well as for special needs (incorporation forms, leasing agreements). You can provide two basic services through your site:

1. Selling various forms, from legal forms to receipt books. These forms will be displayed and sold in your site as any other product: the customer simply selects the form type and the quantity, and receives the form by mail. It is important to include pictures of the various forms you sell.

2. Custom printed forms. The customer uses your site to select the type of form (for example, an invoice), and then enters his name and leaves instructions for the type and size of the font to be used. Logos can either be sent to you through e-mail attachments, fax, or land mail. If you cannot afford printing equipment, consider working with a sub-contractor (however, this may limit your ability to offer attractive deals).

Start-up investment (other than Internet site costs and connection fees): $10,000-$100,000

International potential: None.

Special promotional strategies (in addition to those discussed in chapter 5): Establish links in sites that offer services for businesses. Send direct land mail to small businesses. In the long run, low prices combined with a good, quick service will do more for you than all types of online promotions combined.

Qualifications needed: None.

Educating yourself: Check similar (conventional) businesses and stores to find out what types of forms are in demand and what prices the market will bear.

Number of employees needed to start business (apart from yourself): 0

Things to watch out for: This is a highly competitive business. Your customers will expect fast delivery and meeting deadlines.

Additional income: Labels, signs, stationery, rubber stamps and other business services and products.

Find a similar business at:
http://www.huffman.to/

63. ONLINE ASTROLOGER

Although the credibility of astrology is in doubt, there is no argument that it is a thriving business. People sometimes need to feel that they can get a hold on their lives and even future. Some do so by going to an astrologer or a similar fortune telling service. For them, regardless of the truthfulness of the predictions they hear, these services offer a sense of security and control, relaxation, and happiness — all valuable services to the community.

This is an ideal online business, as it revolves around the exchange of information. The personal touch, however, is all but lost, and has to be made up for by a variety of services and information such as:

1. General astrological forecast. According to their signs, visitors will be able to read or listen to the astrologer's predictions for that week. This should be a free service, as it will attract many visitors to your site.

2. Personal astrological charts. The customer gives you her personal data, and you draw her astrological chart accordingly.

3. One on one consultation through e-mail or chat programs.

4. Books, video and audio cassettes, and similar products for sale.

Start-up investment (other than Internet site costs and connection fees): $1,000-$10,000

International potential: Yes.

Special promotional strategies (in addition to those discussed in chapter 5): Send press releases to astrology, entertainment and general interest magazines. Register your site with every possible directory and online search engine.

Qualifications needed: None.

Educating yourself: Books, publications, courses, seminars.

Number of employees needed to start business (apart from yourself): 0

Things to watch out for: The key to success in this business, even if it is being conducted through chat programs, is personal appeal or charisma. You have to develop a unique edge and character for your site in order to stand out from similar services.

Additional income: Any other form of fortune telling or psychic services.

Find a similar business at:
http://www.webwench.com/astroweb.html

64. EDUCATIONAL PRODUCTS

Educational products, such as correspondence courses or book/cassette courses have always been popular, and the ads promoting them have been a fixture in popular magazines and newspapers for many decades.
   An online center for educational products will help you to cut down significantly on the advertising costs traditionally associated with this business. Visitors to your site will find a (large as possible) selection of

educational products that will cover a vast array of subjects, such as: woodworking, gardening, accounting, algebra, auto mechanics, foreign languages, home inspection, electronics. The courses can be sold in a variety of ways: on video cassettes, books, leaflets, e-mail or land correspondence, CD-ROMs, and more.

You will need to contact the creators of such courses or educational products and probably keep an inventory. In addition, you can develop your own courses or educational packages. This requires an investment of at least $20,000-$30,000 and a tremendous amount of work in research and development. To justify such an investment, you would probably want to market your product through other channels of distribution (other sites, conventional distributors) besides your own site.

Start-up investment (other than Internet site costs and connection fees): $20,000-$100,000

International potential: Yes.

Special promotional strategies (in addition to those discussed in chapter 5): Send press releases to educational, men's and women's magazines, and to magazines that deal with the subject of your courses. Establish links in sites that are likely to be visited by students and young people, or that deal with the subject of your courses.

Qualifications needed: None, but if you decide to develop your own educational product you will need an appropriate background, knowledge and experience in your product's subject matter.

Educating yourself: Learn which courses are in demand. Different courses have different target audiences, and you would want to find out where to reach them — which magazines they read and which sites they frequent.

Number of employees needed to start business (apart from yourself): 0

Things to watch out for: New trends and fads often steer and shape this market. Careers that only yesterday were considered lucrative and hot are often forgotten and ignored a year later.

Additional income: You can develop a unique educational product — a WWW course. For a certain fee, the customer is allowed access to a Web site that functions as the course itself. The customer is led from page to page, and is exposed to: graphics, audio and video files, text, Q&As, tests and, if necessary, e-mail/chat programs.

Find a similar business at: http://www.dickgrove.com

65. REAL ESTATE DATA BASE

Real estate agencies, being of a local nature, require the agent to take potential buyers to see the actual houses they have selected from the agent's brochure. This is something you can never do through the Internet. However, you will be able to share in some of the agents' fees. Your job will be to collect as many of these local brochures into one giant Internet site and to help local agents find potential buyers.

You will work directly with real estate agents from all over the U.S. They will send you their brochures or photographs of houses to be scanned into your site, and you will charge them either a fixed fee for every buyer you send them, or (as they would probably prefer) a percentage of the final sale price.

The photographs in your site are going to be arranged by geographical location, so that people who intend to move to a certain region will be able to view all the houses for sale in that particular region without having to go there in person to collect real estate brochures. Once they have picked a house or several houses from your site, you will give them the relevant agents' addresses and telephone numbers for further contact. This service must be free of charge for visitors to your site in order to attract as many of them as possible and convince real estate agents to work with you. You will make life a lot easier for people who are about to relocate , and especially for those who are not exactly sure where they want to move.

Start-up investment (other than Internet site costs and connection fees): $1,000—$10,000

International potential: None.

Special promotional strategies (in addition to those discussed in chapter 5): Send direct mail and call real estate agents nationwide. Issue press releases to real estate magazines. Word of mouth will be your best promotion, so concentrate on making your selection of houses for sale large and your site user friendly.

Qualifications needed: None.

Number of employees needed to start business (apart from yourself): 0

Things to watch out for: To save space, make the photographs you display on your site no larger than 1½"x 2". If you work with agents from all over the states, your site can easily grow into a mega-site that will require a large, expensive storage space on your server service's computer. You are going to spend a lot of time scanning photographs and updating your site.

Additional income: Offer search services for a fee. For example, a visitor to your site may ask you to find all the colonial houses at a price range of $150,000-250,000 in Connecticut suburbs.

Find a similar business at: http://www.acreage.com

66. RELIGIOUS GOODS CENTER

You can find religious articles and books in almost every household in the world, be its owners religious or secular people. Religious goods, in addition to their ceremonial functions, make good presents and even decorations. Conventional businesses dedicated to selling religious or sacrificial items have existed for thousands of years, from the times of ancient civilizations until today. Religious goods are something that has always been, and for the foreseeable future will always be, in demand.

Services and products visitors will expect to see in your site will include:

1. Religious articles such as menorahs, rosaries, incense, various candles, oils.

2. Custom made items, such as engraved candlesticks, imprinted yarmulkes, altar cloths. You may need to work with sub contractors for these items.

3. Religious books and publications.

4. Gifts — a whole section dedicated to religious gifts, which will be updated and changed according to the current season/holiday. You can include a special children's gifts section, which will concentrate on related games and toys.

5. Free information: lists of gift ideas for specific religious occasions, lists of related businesses (e.g., wedding halls) or organizations, FAQs, description and explanation of religious ceremonies.

Start-up investment (other than Internet site costs and connection fees): $20,000-$100,000

International potential: Yes.

Special promotional strategies (in addition to those discussed in

chapter 5): Establish links in sites that sell gifts or deal with religious topics. When registering your site with search engines, use not only key words relating to religious issues, but also words such as: gift, game, art, engraving, occasion.

Qualifications needed: None.

Educating yourself: You have to learn all you can about the religion or religions you are catering to — customs, ceremonies, holidays, and above all — what articles and books are in popular demand by their followers.

Number of employees needed to start business (apart from yourself): 0

Things to watch out for: Many of the products you are going to sell are seasonal (e.g., Christmas decorations, menorahs). Make sure you are not left with large inventories once the season is ended.

Additional income: Greeting cards with religious themes.

Find a similar business at: http://www.religion-store.com

67. SPORTS MEMORABILIA

Baseball and other sport cards, framed art, plaques, autographed photos and memorabilia, photo key chains, gifts — these and similar items can be sold through a sports memorabilia site. In addition to mainstream sports such as baseball, hockey, football and basketball, you may want to deal with other sports: Indy 500, NASCAR, dirt biking, Grand Prix, and more. The Web allows you to display photographs of your inventory (e.g., rare cards, photos) so that the customer can view your selection, and conventional businesses will have therefore no real advantage over you. Allow visitors to contact you through e-mail and inquire about items your site does not currently display.

You may want to turn this site into a sport center. You can display many kinds of information: game results, game rules, short biographies (of players, coaches, etcetera.), FAQs, and test-your-knowledge quizzes. That way, you will make sure your visitors come back to your site frequently. In addition to the prospect of making money from accepting advertising, repeat customers are more likely (over time) to buy your merchandise.

Start-up investment (other than Internet site costs and connection fees): $20,000-$100,000

International potential: Yes.

Special promotional strategies (in addition to those discussed in chapter 5): Send press releases to sports magazines (emphasize your free information features, not the commercial aspects). Hold sports trivia quizzes. Monitor relevant newsgroups.

Qualifications needed: None.

Educating yourself: You must study the market (through publications, catalogs, market analysis) in order to find out which items are hot and which you should stay away from.

Number of employees needed to start business (apart from yourself): 0

Things to watch out for: Although running this business seems like child's play, thorough knowledge of the market is essential to success and even survival in this market.

Additional income: Selling Hollywood memorabilia.

Find a similar business at: http://www.wwcd.com/a_k/index.html

68. BUSINESS CARDS

Every business needs business cards. This is an ideal Internet business, since ordering a business card is a simple process that can be done in minutes through the customer's computer. First, the customer will choose the paper type his card will be printed on. Next, the text will be entered either through e-mail or a special online form. You will send the customer, through e-mail attachment or fax, a prepared layout for approval, and continue from there. The process can also be automated, i.e. the customer will create the business card himself using your site's special features.

You can either print the cards yourself, which is preferable, or work with a sub contractor, which will make it very hard for you to be price competitive. Delivery is relatively cheap, because cards are packed 500 to a 7"x2"x3½" box. You will be offering one of the most needed business services in the world, and only two things will be required for success: a good price and a user friendly Web site.

Start-up investment (other than Internet site costs and connection fees): $1,000-$50,000

International potential: None.

Special promotional strategies (in addition to those discussed in chapter 5): Send direct land mail to businesses that have an Internet presence (most Internet businesses display their land address on their site). Establish links in sites that offer services for businesses.

Qualifications needed: None.

Educating yourself: The printing machine manufacturer (if you decide to buy one) will probably teach you everything you need to know about the printing process.

Number of employees needed to start business (apart from yourself): 0

Things to watch out for: Buying a new printing machine for a beginning business, before you are sure of success, may not be the best business decision. A good used machine will do the same job for half the price (including repairs) and will not bind you to a long, expensive lease. Pay an experienced printer to teach you how to operate the used machine.

Additional income: Printing receipts, invoices, etc.

Find a similar business at: http://www.americanbiz.com

69. ONLINE SECRETARIAL SERVICES

The majority of small businesses cannot afford the services of a full time secretary. Sometimes, however, these businesses — often a one-person operation — find themselves in dire need of (temporary) secretarial services. Other businesses who may be in need of an outside secretarial service are those whose regular secretary is on vacation or on leave. They can, of course, hire a temp, but often they need only a specific task to be performed, and hiring a temp for an entire day is not cost effective — not when compared to this online service, anyway.

With the click of a button, your customers can gain access to several secretarial services. For example, typing and word processing services. The customer dictates a letter through a chat program, and you type it. The finished document can either be sent to the customer via e-mail, or forwarded to its intended destination. Your site will consist of a simple homepage that will list the services you offer, your rates, and an e-mail contact or the chat/Internet telephony program where you can be reached.

Start-up investment (other than Internet site costs and connection fees): $1,000-$5,000

International potential: Yes. You will perform an important service for business people who are abroad on a business trip and who do not have a secretary with them, or those who would like to send letters to domestic companies from abroad.

Special promotional strategies (in addition to those discussed in chapter 5): Establish links in sites that offer services for businesses. Send press releases to business and trade magazines.

Qualifications needed: Typing skills, shorthand.

Educating yourself: Short, simple courses or even educational computer software (e.g., one that teaches typing).

Number of employees needed to start business (apart from yourself): 0

Things to watch out for: Since many of your clients will require a copy of the letters they dictate on floppy disks, you may need to purchase several word processors or be able to convert your files into a format compatible with your client's word processor. This type of business will require you to remain close to your Internet connection at all times in case a client needs an immediate service.

Additional income: Translation services.

Find a similar business at:
http://www.mobileword.com/mwhome.htm

70. ELDERLY CARE SERVICE

Upon reaching a certain age, a great number of senior citizens find (usually to their horror) that they can no longer take care of themselves; that they are no longer fully independent. They and their families are not always aware of their options, and careful planning often gives way to panic, depression and an inevitable feeling of guilt for both parent and child.

This site will serve to educate the elderly and their families, reassure them, and make clear the options they have before them. You will have to deal with two main issues:

1. Care for the elderly in their own homes. This will include referring the client to nursing services or special therapists, and recommending certain items (e.g., walking aids) for the elderly. You will also help them find recreational activities they can participate in and services that will help them reduce their dependency on their family members (a special taxi service, for instance). In addition, establish a consultation service to answer the senior citizen's family's questions about daily care and health problems.

2. Taking care of the elderly in a nursing home. You can provide a referral service for nursing homes. The list of nursing homes you display must be rated and any special problems, disadvantages or benefits that any of the nursing homes mentioned there might have must be made clear to your customers.

Your income can be derived from consultation fees, referral fees (you have to reach an agreement with the businesses you recommend), and from the selling of health or special aid items online.

Start-up investment (other than Internet site costs and connection fees): $1,000-$50,000

International potential: None.

Special promotional strategies (in addition to those discussed in chapter 5): Establish links in sites that deal with health or geriatric issues. Issue press releases to health and family oriented magazines. Send direct mail to senior citizens' organizations.

Qualifications needed: The advantages of a background in elderly care and health services cannot be underestimated.

Educating yourself: You will need to compile a list of all the day care services and elder homes throughout the U.S., and look for publications and magazines that describe and rate them.

Number of employees needed to start business (apart from yourself): 0

Things to watch out for: Make sure you do not recommend nursing homes and similar businesses according to the referral fee they are willing to pay you. Such a practice, aside from being immoral, will earn your business a bad reputation that will stifle its growth if not even destroy it completely in a very short time.

Additional income: Selling special aids for the disabled. Internet consultation for senior citizens.

Find a similar business at: http://www.retirenet.com

71. AUCTION AND SURPLUS SALE CENTER

Most of us like to go to auctions or sealed bids. You can pay as low as one tenth of the actual value of any item sold, and you can buy things you could never afford otherwise. You can even become a dealer and resell these items to retailers or to the public. The problem for most people is that they can only read auction notices in their own local papers, while excellent opportunities may await in other parts of the country almost every week.

What auction goers need is access to two kinds of information: a weekly list of all the important auctions nationwide, and instructions on how to get on government mailing lists.

Information of the first category must be arranged by subject. For example: automobile auctions. For a nominal fee, an annual subscription or (if you want to base your income on accepting advertising) for free, you will allow customers access to every important auction (not "content of a grocery store") published in a U.S. newspaper.

To get on a government mailing list (i.e. to receive information about government surplus sales and auctions), the customer will first have to purchase an information package from you. In it, you will give the customer the addresses of government agencies (e.g., the U.S. Customs Service, Department of Defense), explain the different classes of property for sale and their special codes, and provide the appropriate request forms for the above agencies.

Start-up investment (other than Internet site costs and connection fees): $1,000-$5,000

International potential: Yes.

Special promotional strategies (in addition to those discussed in chapter 5): Many of your customers will be people who did not even know this kind of business existed before they arrived at your site. For this reason, the key words you will use to list your business in search engines should include not only words such as "auction," but also: bargain, deal, sale, garage sale, bid, discount, business opportunity, cheap, money, save. Send press releases to regional and men's magazines.

Qualifications needed: None.

Educating yourself: Order a few information packages from similar businesses. Subscribe to relevant newspapers, publications and mailing lists.

Number of employees needed to start business (apart from yourself): 0

Things to watch out for: Make sure at least some of the services in your site are free. Most people will not realize what they can gain by bidding at auctions until they see examples from previous auctions that reflect the huge offering of goods that is out there (and the prices they go for). Auction notices on your site will have to be updated every week. You may need to get permission from the newspapers whose ads you are displaying on your site.

Additional income: Hold auctions yourself: for a certain fee, you will help Internet users auction off various items on your site.

Find a similar business at: http://www.internetliquidators.com

72. ONLINE TUTOR

Many, if not most pupils need a tutor to help them in at least one or two subjects. Not everyone, however, can afford it, and some students are living in remote rural areas where travel time makes personal tutor visits impractical.

An online tutor can be reached from anywhere in the world, and his services can be used for short or long periods. For example, a pupil who has difficulties in understanding the reasons for the fall of Ancient Rome and whose family cannot afford a tutor may take only two or three online lessons to cover this particular subject.

You will work with your students via chat/Internet telephony programs, which will utilize both audio and text capabilities. In addition, you can use e-mail or special online forms that your site will feature. Your fee should be slightly lower than that of a conventional tutor, since no travel is involved and certain limitations exist (e.g., you can't check the students' school notebooks unless they have a scanner). This lower fee, however, will most certainly be a major factor in parents' decision to use your services.

Start-up investment (other than Internet site costs and connection fees): $1,000-$5,000

International potential: Yes (for children of families who are staying abroad for a long period of time).

Special promotional strategies (in addition to those discussed in chapter 5): Send direct land mail to school newspaper editors and community centers. Establish links in sites that deal with education and parenting. Some of your students, who do not have computers or Internet access at home, will be referred to your service by an educator, and will probably use the school's computers to connect to your site. It is important, therefore, to promote your business in teachers' circles.

Qualifications needed: Teaching experience will lend credibility to your business and help you promote it.

Educating yourself: Textbooks, teaching guides, publications and magazines dealing with education, seminars.

Number of employees needed to start business (apart from yourself): 0

Things to watch out for: Sometimes, you may be dealing not only with the students' difficulties with the subject you are teaching, but also with their motivational, social and even family problems. There's more to teaching than just reading textbooks to the students.

Additional income: Offer help in home assignments — answer a few specific questions in the area of your expertise.

Find a similar business at:
http://www.netsrq.com/~hahn/calc.html

73. TOURIST INFORMATION CENTER

This site will help tourists to plan their visit to the U.S. (or other countries) efficiently and conveniently. This must be a large, yet user friendly site that will enable the user to choose the states or cities they intend to visit, and receive a list of hotels, motels, car rentals, bicycle rentals, casino resorts and various tourist attractions in that area. Every resort on the list should include a short description, as well as your own remarks or ratings that will give your business its unique character and help create that craved word of mouth publicity. In addition, offer links to related sites.

Your income will be generated from four sources:

1. Referral fees charged from the resorts on your list.

2. Accepting advertising.

3. Consultation. Through e-mail, some future tourists may ask you to plan a route for them, supply more information on a certain resort or city, or provide other additional information that is not on the list (e.g., ask you to find museums of aviation on the east coast).

4. Selling tourist guides, travel books, and maps online.

Start-up investment (other than Internet site costs and connection fees): $1,000-$5,000

International potential: Yes.

Special promotional strategies (in addition to those discussed in chapter 5): Establish links in online travel agencies' sites and popular foreign sites (even foreign language sites). Send press releases to foreign touring and travel magazines. Send direct land mail to foreign tourist supply shops and ask them to post your online address on their notice board (most of these stores have a special notice board for travelers who are looking for traveling companions, camping equipment for sale, etcetera). Contact publishers of tourist guides and ask them to mention your online business in their books (they will probably charge you a fee for this).

Qualifications needed: None.

Educating yourself: Tourist guides and relevant publications. Contact the resorts you intend to list in your site and ask them a series of questions (e.g., about access for people with disabilities, rates) that will allow you to display helpful information in your site.

Number of employees needed to start business (apart from yourself): 0

Things to watch out for: The information you display on your site must be up-to-date in order to give you an edge over conventional competitors. For example, if you know that a major rock concert is about to be held in Philadelphia in two months, dedicate a special part of your site to hotels and other resorts in that region, and include detailed information about hotel vacancy and availability of cars for rent before and during the concert.

Additional income: Online souvenir shop.

Find a similar business at: http://www.expedia.com

74. ONLINE TRAVEL AGENCY

This business combines low start up costs with a high profit potential. You will have to work in collaboration with an established travel agency for a commission at first, and hook up to their computer network. Many travel agencies are willing to work with outside agents on a commission basis, and some even encourage this.

As an online travel agent, you will enable customers from all over the world to book airline tickets and put together tour packages to any destination on the globe from their own PCs. You will also handle hotel, train, bus, and car rental reservations, and special packages such as cruises, club med, honeymoon or group tours.

To promote your site, you may want to dedicate a large part of it to free information. Such information can include lists of resorts (see: Tourist Information Center), FAQs, links to related sites (not rival travel agencies, of course) and more. You will also have to allow your customers to contact you through chat/Internet telephony or at least e-mail should the need arise.

Start-up investment (other than Internet site costs and connection fees): $1,000-$20,000

International potential: Yes.

Special promotional strategies (in addition to those discussed in chapter 5): Establish links in sites that deal with entertainment, transportation or tourism. When registering your site with search engines, use every key word that may attract people to your site; not only words such as: travel, vacation, leisure, hotel; but also: joy, relaxation, betterment, therapy, depression, self-help.

Qualifications needed: Some travel agencies will require you to go to a travel industry course.

Educating yourself: Courses, seminars, literature, publications, and consultation with the travel agency you work with.

Number of employees needed to start business (apart from yourself): 0

Things to watch out for: This is a highly competitive business.

Additional income: Selling tourist guides and other tourist items on your site.

Find a similar business at: http://www.arctic.net/~airtn

75. WEDDING CENTER

People who are about to get married, and especially their parents, spend a lot of money on the occasion. This money goes to a variety of services and products — all of which you can either offer or represent in your site:

1. A referral service for: photographers/video, disc jockeys, bands, caterers, wedding cakes, florists, limousines, honeymoon travels, wedding halls, beauty salons, shoes, tuxedos, tents and chairs.

2. A virtual shop for such items as: jewelry, headpieces and veils, balloons, glassware, haberdashery, religious goods.

3. Wedding invitations. The customer can use special forms on your site to enter text and choose font size and style, type of paper, and quantity. The invitations can either be delivered to the customer or, for an additional fee, be sent directly to their destinations.

4. Consultation service (help with the planning of the wedding) through e-mail or chat/Internet telephony programs.

Start-up investment (other than Internet site costs and connection fees): $20,000-$100,000

International potential: None.

Special promotional strategies (in addition to those discussed in chapter 5): When registering your site with a search engine, use key words pertaining to all the businesses and services mentioned in the four above categories individually. Send press releases to general interest and women's magazines.

Qualifications needed: None, but experience in organizing weddings is a must.

Educating yourself: Compile a list of reputable businesses throughout the U.S. Read every possible book and publication on planning and organizing weddings.

Number of employees needed to start business (apart from yourself): 0

Things to watch out for: When building your inventory, don't invest in items that people would never buy online, such as wedding gowns.

Additional income: You can offer similar services for proms, sweet sixteens, bar mitzvahs, christenings and other occasions in your site.

Find a similar business at:
http://members.aol.com/weddlinks/index.html

76. RARE BOOKS/RECORDS FINDER

When people suddenly remember a book or record they once had or heard about and they can't find it in an ordinary book or record store, they sometimes develop an obsession with it; money is often no object. People need these books and records for their collections, for nostalgic reasons or simply because of a sudden interest they have in the rare object's subject matter or creator.

Your site can be very simple, and only one to two Web pages in length. All the customer need do is key in the title of the book or record they are looking for, as well as any additional data they have on it. Fees will be determined by the rarity of the object. You can either provide your customer with the name and address of the dealer you found the book or record at, or order it for her yourself. You can also become a rare book/record dealer and invest in an inventory.

Start-up investment (other than Internet site costs and connection fees): $1,000-$100,000 (with inventory).

International potential: Yes. In fact, for some people you may be the only hope of finding a rare book/record without having to make the trip to your country themselves.

Special promotional strategies (in addition to those discussed in chapter 5): People who are obsessed with finding a rare object will leave no stone unturned in their search for it, and that includes the Internet. For that reason, registering your site with every possible search engine and under as many relevant key words as possible is of a vital importance. Send press releases to literary, music, and entertainment magazines. Establish links in sites that sell books and CDs (new and used) or that deal with the music industry, collectors, literary issues and even poetry.

Qualifications needed: None.

Educating yourself: Books, catalogs, online lists, publications dedicated to the used book/record trade.

Number of employees needed to start business (apart from yourself): 0

Things to watch out for: Since only a few of the rare book/record stores and dealers you will have to contact have an online presence (as of today, anyway) expect long distance calls to be a substantial item of your operating costs. It will take you some time to network and to learn different dealers' areas of speciality, but when you do your search time will be drastically reduced.

Additional income: Rare comic books.

Find a similar business at:
http://members.aol.com/MCRecords/index.htm

77. UNIQUE OUTDOOR ACTIVITIES CENTER

Often, people find themselves getting bored of the same: work—vacation in some resort—work—vacation in some resort—work routine. They want a new experience, an adventure to remember. They want something different.

In your site, you can book and arrange: hot air balloon rides, hang gliding courses, back country activities, snowmobile tours, climbing, skydiving, spelunking, orienteering, scuba diving, whale watching, and even unique experiences such as WWII vintage airplane rides. As these activities do not always spring to mind when planning a vacation, it is your site's job to make people aware of their existence by displaying graphics, photos, and enthusiastic descriptions of each activity. You will also need to assuage people's fears (especially of skydiving and hang gliding) by displaying statistics or articles written by prominent experts in those fields.

Your income will be derived from a referral service for organizers of the above activities, as well as from selling related items on your site (guidebooks, basic equipment such as compasses or sleeping bags, etcetera).

Start-up investment (other than Internet site costs and connection fees): $1,000-$50,000

International potential: Yes.

Special promotional strategies (in addition to those discussed in chapter 5): Send press releases to travel and hobby magazines. Include key words such as "travel agent" in your search engine listings so that even people who are looking for conventional vacations will be referred to your site. Establish links in sites that deal with the travel industry, sports, camping, entertainment.

Qualifications needed: None.

Educating yourself: Publications and directories that list

organizers of outdoor activities.

Number of employees needed to start business (apart from yourself): 0

Things to watch out for: Convincing people to try a new adventure they have never considered before is the key to success in this business, and your site's main task. Dedicate time and effort to creating an appealing, graphically pleasing site that will have something for everyone, and which will offer a lot of free information and gimmicks to ensure repeat visitors. Remember — customers may visit your site up to five or six times before deciding on using one of your "crazy" activities.

Additional income: You can start a database of people who are interested in forming groups for touring and other outdoor activities. You can charge either a nominal fee from people who buy a space on this list, or make it a free service to enhance your main business.

Find a similar business at: http://www.w-o-w.com

78. RECIPE CENTER

This type of business is based on the transfer of text-based data, which can easily be downloaded through e-mail or simply printed from your site. This makes it an ideal online business.

In order to attract users to your site, you have to include hundreds of free recipes (preferably with photographs attached). Allow users to post their own recipes in a special section of your site. Your income will be generated from:

1. Special recipes for sale. Once the users have exhausted all available free recipes on your site, the gourmets and food-lovers among them will be interested in any special, exotic recipes not

easily found elsewhere. You can sell these either in packages (e.g., West Indies' cooking) or one by one.

2. Consultation. Answering cooking questions, and solving problems in real time. This can also be promoted as a "cooking disaster hot line."

3. Online cooking school. You can sell step by step instructions for beginners through e-mail, or sell courses on video cassettes.

4. A virtual shop for cookbooks, kitchenware, etcetera.

Start-up investment (other than Internet site costs and connection fees): $1,000-$15,000

International potential: Yes.

Special promotional strategies (in addition to those discussed in chapter 5): Establish links in sites that cater to gourmets. Send press releases to food and drink magazines. Monitor relevant newsgroups.

Qualifications needed: Cooking skills.

Educating yourself: Recipes can be found in magazines, cookbooks (including old, forgotten cookbooks), online resources. Make sure they are not copyrighted. Exchange recipes with other gourmets and cooks/chefs.

Number of employees needed to start business (apart from yourself): 0

Things to watch out for: There are thousands of sites out there that offer free recipes. You must be unique to stand out from the crowd.

Additional income: A referral service for cooking schools.

Find a similar business at: http://www.pazsaz.com/pattye.html

79. KIT CENTER

As anyone who has ever read magazines such as *Popular Mechanics, Popular Science* or *Plane & Pilot* knows, the kit industry is a thriving and diversified one. Almost every mechanical or electronic product on the market also exists in the form of a kit — airplanes, cars, stereo systems, boats. Many unique products exist only as kits — mini submarines, small helicopters, performance boosters for car/bike engines and more. Some of these kits sell only in the form of plans, requiring the customer to look for the parts himself, while others sell in a complete package.

There are three ways to sell kits:

1. As any other product: you keep an inventory and send the customer the kit he selected from your site.

2. By drop shipment. Working on a commission basis, you contact the kit's manufacturer and have him send it to the customer.

3. Online. If you are selling only plans or formulas, you can have them sent to the customer via e-mail attachment, or simply allow him to print them directly from your site.

Start-up investment (other than Internet site costs and connection fees): $1,000-$100,000

International potential: Yes.

Special promotional strategies (in addition to those discussed in chapter 5): Send press releases to hobby and craft, automotive, motorcycle, aviation, and science magazines. Establish links in sites that deal with hobbies, tools, mechanics, electronics. Make sure you have a few irresistible, unbelievable kits to help attract users to your site (e.g., a laser gun, a listening-through-walls device).

Qualifications needed: None.

Educating yourself: Look through every magazine that deals with mechanics or electronics. Contact the kit manufacturers (some of them are very small one-product companies) you find there.

Number of employees needed to start business (apart from yourself): 0

Things to watch out for: Check the kit manufacturers' products before you display them on your site. Some make fraudulent or misleading claims about their products (especially concerning the investment in time and money needed to build the kit).

Additional income: Selling toy kits (model airplanes, ships). Selling related books and video cassettes.

Find a similar business at:
http://www.aerocompinc.com/

80. PAGERS

The simplicity and speed of transactions in this business will make it easy for you to design a fully automated site. You will need to work with local paging services from different parts of the U.S. (many of the paging services work mainly through local agents). The beepers you sell can have a local, regional or nationwide coverage. The paging systems can be numeric or text based.

Your site will be simple and small. You need to supply the visitors with pricing, fees (usually annual), delivery and product information, and present them with an online form they can fill in with their personal data. The pager will be sent to them either by you or by the local paging service.

Start-up investment (other than Internet site costs and connection fees): $1,000-$5,000

International potential: None.

Special promotional strategies (in addition to those discussed in chapter 5): Establish links in sites that deal with telecommunication, services for businesses, and electronic equipment. When registering with search engines, make sure that the first lines written in your site (those which are displayed for search engine users), or preferably your site's title and Meta file, will convey the good deals you offer on pagers — the major, if not only, reason anyone would visit your site.

Qualifications needed: None.

Educating yourself: Visit a few selling points for pagers (off-line and online) and learn what deals or extras they offer their customers.

Number of employees needed to start business (apart from yourself): 0

Things to watch out for: This is a highly competitive business, since anyone can start it with just a minimal investment.

Additional income: Cellular phones.

Find a similar business at:
http://members.aol.com/novetek/index.html

81. ONLINE PRIVATE INVESTIGATOR

As a P.I., you can use your site for two purposes:

1. To promote your conventional business in the local community. You will provide all the services a conventional private investigator would, and the Internet will become just another

means of promotion for your conventional office.

2. To create a true online business. This means that you cannot meet personally with your clients, arrive at their homes/businesses, or offer services such as surveillance. On the other hand, you will have a nationwide appeal, and can expect to serve a much larger audience. You can take cases that require networking, computers, and access to databases. Such cases may include searching for missing persons, background investigations, asset searches, computer searches, pre-marital checks. You can also work with local sub contractors, such as photographers and other investigators.

You can also, of course, combine the two approaches, and let your Internet site supplement your existing business.

Your site will be simple, functioning only as a contact point for the customer, who will speak to you through chat/Internet telephony programs or e-mail.

Start-up investment (other than Internet site costs and connection fees): $1,000-$5,000

International potential: Yes (if your overseas customer asks you to find out information about people or corporations in the U.S.).

Special promotional strategies (in addition to those discussed in chapter 5): Send press releases to business, trade, and general interest magazines. Establish links in sites that offer services for businesses, or that deal with marital problems.

Qualifications needed: Some states require a license for conducting certain investigations. A background in law enforcement is a definite plus.

Educating yourself: Courses, literature, working as an apprentice or as a police detective.

Number of employees needed to start business (apart from

yourself): 0

Things to watch out for: High telephone bills.

Additional income: Running an online spy shop: debugging devices, microphones, etcetera.

Find a similar business at:
http://www.france-investigation.com/jcs3.htm

82. BUSINESS PLAN WRITING SERVICE

Anyone who has ever sought start-up capital for a new business knows that lenders usually ask for a business plan. A professionally written business plan outlines for the lender the applicant's projected expenses, income, business approaches and, in general — his chances of succeeding in the planned business. A business plan also gives the lender an accurate picture of the lender's business skills (being realistic, good planning, knowledge and understanding of promotional tactics).

Since a business plan is one of the most important documents any new business needs to produce, business owners usually hire professionals to prepare it for them. Fees are very high in this business (several thousand dollars for an average business plan), and thousands of new potential clients enter the market every day.

To attract visitors to your site, consider dedicating a few Web pages to free information, links and FAQs.

Start-up investment (other than Internet site costs and connection fees): $1,000-$5,000

International potential: Yes (for foreign businesspeople who are looking to invest in the U.S.A.).

Special promotional strategies (in addition to those discussed in

chapter 5): Establish links in sites that provide services for businesses and in those that deal with financing. Offer lenders and CPAs a referral fee for every customer they send you.

Qualifications needed: Business skills and some experience in working with lenders.

Educating yourself: Books, software, courses, working for a lender or a business plan writer.

Number of employees needed to start business (apart from yourself): 0

Things to watch out for: Not every business, of course, succeeds in being approved for a loan. When this happens, some of the would-be new business owners abandon the idea, and with it any financial obligations the new business might have. If you are not sure of your client's integrity, consider charging for your services in advance (or at least take 50% up front).

Additional income: Selling related software, books, info packages. Other services for businesses.

Find a similar business at: http://bulletproofbizplans.com

83. ONLINE MODELING AGENCY

Starting a modeling agency requires little investment, but excellent talent scouting and marketing skills. You have two main jobs:

1. Finding the right models to represent. Finding wannabe models is very easy; finding ones that are likely to be hired is quite another matter. In addition to good (or great) looks, the candidate must also have good communicative skills (e.g., for trade show

presentations), know how to carry herself in a showroom, etcetera.

2. Searching for customers who will hire your models. These may be mega stores, malls, advertisers, organizers of local events, exhibitions, trade shows, fashion designers and others. You will reach them either the conventional way — direct mail, telephone — or let them and many other businesses find your Web site. Either way, you will direct their attention to online portfolios of the models you represent, which will include several high-grade photos and the model's personal data. Should they request it, you will of course mail potential customers a copy of the portfolio, but for most, a quick browse through your site will be more than enough to determine whether or not any of the models is right for them. You can also include video/audio samples in these portfolios to help the potential customer evaluate the candidate's skills (e.g., if they need her to announce new products they will probably be interested in the model's voice).

Another source of income for you is charging aspiring models for displaying their portfolios on your site. However, make sure not to create an overabundance of such portfolios to the point of diluting the important core of excellent models you have chosen yourself. Potential customers must be made aware of the difference between the two groups.

Start-up investment (other than Internet site costs and connection fees): $1,000-$5,000

International potential: None.

Special promotional strategies (in addition to those discussed in chapter 5): To attract models: establish links in sites that appeal to young people and teenagers. Send press releases to magazines that deal with similar subject matters. To convince models (other than those you have chosen to represent) to display their portfolios on your site for a fee, you would want your site to show as much traffic as possible. Consider offering free services to visitors in order to achieve this. To find employment for your models: establish links in sites that sell services for businesses or that deal with advertising and promotion. Send press releases to general interest, fashion, trade, and regional magazines.

Qualifications needed: None.

Educating yourself: Books, publications, magazines. Study the market and learn what potential customers are looking for in a model.

Number of employees needed to start business (apart from yourself): 0

Things to watch out for: Consult a lawyer before drafting the contracts you want your models to sign.

Additional income: A referral service for modeling schools and portfolio photographers.

Find a similar business at: http://www.newfaces.com/index.html

84. LIFE/DISABILITY INSURANCE

An online insurance business can either take care of the entire process for the customer (applications, filling forms, taking payment), which means becoming an agent and being affiliated with an insurance company, or it can act as a link or a referral service to established agents.

Your site could offer visitors free information, quotes (this is very important!), FAQ's, and an e-mail address for inquiries. You can also sell other forms of insurance (for example, health insurance) and construct your site accordingly, with related statistics and links to sites that deal with health issues.

Start-up investment (other than Internet site costs and connection fees): $1,000-$10,000

International potential: None.

Special promotional strategies (in addition to those discussed in chapter 5): Concentrate on low rates (yours or of the agents you represent), and make them known to the public. Your site's title — the first and sometimes only description of it people will see while using search engines — must convey this message. Press releases for this type of business will probably not interest editors unless you think of an additional, unique service to offer in your site.

Qualifications needed: License (if you act as an insurance agent).

Educating yourself: Courses, books.

Number of employees needed to start business (apart from yourself): 0

Things to watch out for: This is a highly competitive business. However, your low overhead will allow you to work on a smaller commission and to offer better deals than conventional agents.

Additional income: A referral service for local low-rate auto insurance agencies.

Find a similar business at: http://www.quotesmith.com

85. USED COMPUTERS BROKER

Almost every Internet user owns a computer. Computers are constantly replaced and upgraded, and this creates a vibrant, ever growing market for used computers and accessories.

You can do the following on your site:

1. Act as a broker — you will buy used computers and computer accessories and sell them through your site.

2. Charge sellers a nominal fee for online classified ads that you will display on your site. You can also charge them a percentage of the advertised prices, which means that the ad will run until the item is sold.

3. Allow customers to advertise the used computers they have for sale free of charge, leaving you with an income from accepting commercial advertising and from mediating services (the buyer sends the money to you and you forward it to the seller as soon as the buyer receives the item by mail).

You may want to offer various free services on your site in order to attract visitors: troubleshooting guides, suggested price list for used computer equipment, etcetera.

Start-up investment (other than Internet site costs and connection fees): $1,000-$50,000

International potential: Yes (where there are no customs restrictions).

Special promotional strategies (in addition to those discussed in chapter 5): Send press releases to computer and youth oriented magazines. As almost every Internet user owns a computer, any link to any Internet site will be as good as the next — here's where you can concentrate on the quantity rather than the quality of links. Monitor relevant newsgroups.

Qualifications needed: None, but a background in computers will be very helpful.

Educating yourself: Computer hardware books and courses. Study the computer market. Find out where and when auctions for used computer equipment are being held (major newspapers usually advertise several of these every week).

Number of employees needed to start business (apart from yourself): 0

Things to watch out for: Even if you allow visitors to post their classified ads free of charge, retain control of the ads' content. They must deal only with computer equipment, not with other equipment or appliances, or your site will lose its unique edge.

Additional income: Referral service for local repair shops.

Find a similar business at:
http://www.holcroftb.demon.co.uk

86. HOME MADE CRAFTS

Selling home made items will give you great flexibility in matters such as inventory, costs, quality control, availability of items. It is a far more creative, fun and satisfying business than selling ready made products. Home made crafts are great for gifts, decorations and even practical purposes (e.g., fishing tackles). Here is a list of some of the products and crafts you can make at home:

- ❒ Bird feeders
- ❒ Ornamental bird cages
- ❒ Ceramics
- ❒ Shell products (e.g., lamps)
- ❒ Quilts
- ❒ Flower pictures
- ❒ Origami models
- ❒ Rugs
- ❒ Dolls and miniatures
- ❒ Whittling
- ❒ Buttons
- ❒ Mobiles

❏ Rock arrangements
❏ Wreaths

You will need to display photographs of your best samples on your site (you will probably want to hire the services of a professional photographer to take these pictures, because they will be an important factor in the customer's decision as to whether or not to purchase the crafts).

Start-up investment (other than Internet site costs and connection fees): $2,000-$10,000

International potential: Yes.

Special promotional strategies (in addition to those discussed in chapter 5): Send press releases to hobby and craft, house and garden, general interest, and other relevant magazines (according to the items you sell). Link to and from sites that deal with the gift industry. If you decide to invest in paid advertising, concentrate your efforts around the holiday seasons.

Qualifications needed: None.

Educating yourself: Books and courses dealing with the individual crafts you intend to manufacture.

Number of employees needed to start business (apart from yourself): 0

Things to watch out for: While it is important to choose the crafts you love to make, be sure they are in demand first.

Additional income: Selling literature about crafts and hobbies (especially how-to books).

Find a similar business at:
http://www.keepsakes-ceramics.com/index.htm

87. PORTRAIT PAINTING FROM PHOTOGRAPHS

The concept is simple — your clients will send you their photographs, and you will paint a portrait from these photographs according to their instructions, and mail it back to them. This business hinges upon talent and marketing skills only, and requires a very little start-up investment. You can either paint the portraits yourself or work with local painters (especially young, struggling artists who will be more than happy to see some of their work being sold).

The first thing users who visit your site must see are samples indicative of your talent as a painter. The samples should show both the portrait and the photo it was taken from. Next, they should be given information about your prices, delivery time, and the options they have (size, canvas or paper, black and white or color). The photographs can be sent to you as e-mail attachments or simply by land mail. In addition to portraits, you can of course paint buildings, landscape, and anything else that the customer submits a photograph of.

Start-up investment (other than Internet site costs and connection fees): $1,000-$5,000

International potential: Yes.

Special promotional strategies (in addition to those discussed in chapter 5): Establish links in sites that deal with art, gifts, decorations, interior designing (people who move into a new home or who are renovating an existing one are likely to invest in paintings). Register your site not only under the key words: portrait, painting; but also under words such as: gift, birthday, holiday, wallpaper, furniture, home, family.

Qualifications needed: None.

Educating yourself: Learning to paint portraits is not as hard as it might seem, but it does take some practice before you will be able to offer your services to the public.

Number of employees needed to start business (apart from yourself): 0

Things to watch out for: Charge at least 30-40% up front before you take any job. Don't be too price competitive or people will get the impression that you are an amateur.

Additional income: A restoration service (for old, faded or partially destroyed paintings). Custom frames.

Find a similar business at: http://www.classic1.demon.co.uk/

88. AUTO TRANSPORT/DRIVE-AWAY

According to statistics, the average American family moves to a new home every four years. Many of these families move to a remote place, and not everyone is enthusiastic about the prospect of driving his own car for thousands of miles. There are two ways an auto transport business can help such individuals: by transporting the car on a special truck, or by sending it via drive-away. The latter method involves sending the car with a driver (usually a tourist) who has until a certain date (no more than 5-10 days) to deliver the car to its owner. This driver is not paid for transporting the car, because he is benefitting from this service himself by saving money on travel expenses.

You can provide the transportation service yourself and deal with drivers and customers, or you can refer both to local auto transport businesses and charge the latter a fee. You may want to set up an automated quote system and FAQs in your site that will relieve you from some of the most common inquiries visitors are likely to e-mail to you.

Start-up investment (other than Internet site costs and connection fees): $1,000-$5,000

International potential: None.

Special promotional strategies (in addition to those discussed in chapter 5): To reach potential drive-away drivers: establish links in sites (including foreign sites) that are frequented by tourists and travelers. Contact publishers of tourist guides and ask them to mention your online business in their books (they will probably charge you a fee for this). Send direct land mail to foreign tourist supply shops and ask them to post your online address on their store's notice board. To reach potential customers: establish links in sites that deal with moving, services for home owners, job search, mortgage brokers. Register your site with search engines under key words pertaining to these subjects.

Qualifications needed: None.

Educating yourself: Get the telephone numbers of all local auto transport companies and reach a referral fee agreement with them.

Number of employees needed to start business (apart from yourself): 0

Things to watch out for: Make sure the local businesses you work with have proper insurance. If you decide to provide the service yourself rather than be a referral service: drivers have to qualify and hold a either a valid U.S. license or a valid foreign license with an international permit; take a deposit ($100-$200) from each driver and passenger.

Additional income: Transporting cars for car dealerships (special orders, auctions). Shipping cars overseas.

Find a similar business at: http://www.csaf.org/transon

89. USED CAR CENTER

You, too, can lay claim to some of the tens of billions of dollars that change hands every year in used car transactions. People who buy used cars often spend money also on: car parts and accessories, auto mechanics, insurance companies, consumer reports, paint and body shops, auto loan brokers, diagnostics services, auction fees, car manuals and literature, classified ads, credit repair services, performance equipment, wax and wash, alarm systems and locking devices.

You can generate your income from any, or a combination of the above businesses. On your site, visitors may find a virtual shop (especially for car accessories), a referral service, or a consultation service, but you will also have to give these visitors some free services to boost your business. For example, old model reports, statistics, tips for buyers and sellers, auction information, FAQs. If, for instance, you have decided to open a virtual shop for car manuals, technical guides and related literature, it might be a very good idea to include a free online automobile classified ad board (divided according to regions) to attract visitors. You can also try to charge a nominal fee for every ad, but customers will most likely prefer to spend their advertising money on local papers.

Start-up investment (other than Internet site costs and connection fees): $1,000-$100,000

International potential: Yes.

Special promotional strategies (in addition to those discussed in chapter 5): Send press releases to local used car market press (who might accept it if you agree to include some of their classified ads in your site). This is a business of general appeal, so links should be established in high traffic sites, and not necessarily in ones that specialize in the automotive industry.

Qualifications needed: None.

Educating yourself: Contact local businesses (if you want to start a referral service). Study the market of the specific service/item you have chosen.

Number of employees needed to start business (apart from yourself): 0

Things to watch out for: Don't try to include the whole spectrum of related auto-industry businesses mentioned above under your site. Concentrate on one or two services (e.g., car accessories, referral service for paint and body shops) and switch to other services only in case those fail to live up to your expectations.

Additional income: A center for used boats, bikes, RVs.

Find a similar business at: http://www.manheim.com (this site deals mainly with auto auctions).

90. QUIT SMOKING CENTER

About 15 percent of the American population, and a similar or higher percentage in most other countries are smokers. The vast majority of smokers would like to stop smoking, but for most it is a continuous, intolerable test of will power. Still, smokers are always on the lookout for new methods of quitting, and those with an Internet access are most likely to drop by a site that deals with this problem.

You can offer these visitors the following:

1. One on one consultation service through e-mail or Internet telephony programs.

2. Free information — statistics, advice, various methods of quitting, FAQs, related health problems and how to treat them, general health information. You can also include visitors' own contributions (advice, quitting stories) in a special Web page.

3. A referral service for local clinics (e.g., for acupunctive treatment, hypnotists).

4. A virtual shop for related products (such as nicotine patches) and literature.

Start-up investment (other than Internet site costs and connection fees): $1,000-$20,000

International potential: Yes.

Special promotional strategies (in addition to those discussed in chapter 5): Smoking is a widespread problem, so any link and press release will probably reach your potential customers. Make sure you are registered with every possible search engine, and monitor relevant newsgroups (or possibly start your own).

Qualifications needed: None.

Educating yourself: Books, publications, seminars.

Number of employees needed to start business (apart from yourself): 0

Things to watch out for: The commercial aspects of your site must be downplayed. This must be a free information, public service site in order to attract visitors.

Additional income: Alcoholism treatment center.

Find a similar business at: http://www.chriscor.com/linkstoa.htm

91. LANDSCAPE AND GARDEN CENTER

As an online landscape consultant you will not be able to come to people's houses to do the landscape job yourself, but you will be able to offer help in the designing of the landscape and in acquiring the necessary tools and plants. You will deal with trees, shrubs, mulch, flowers, sod, tree removal, house plants, lawn, rock gardens, pruning, peat moss, soil quality, and maintenance. Your site should consist of:

1. Free information, advice and how-to.

2. A designing/consultation services. The customers will send you photographs of their yard, and discuss (via chat programs or Internet telephony) their plans with you.

3. A virtual storefront. You can sell seeds, bulbs, tools, literature.

4. A referral service for local landscape contractors. After all, the do-it-yourself approach is not for everyone.

Start-up investment (other than Internet site costs and connection fees): $10,000-$50,000

International potential: Yes (but there may be limitations on the selling of plants and seeds).

Special promotional strategies (in addition to those discussed in chapter 5): Establish links in sites that deal with real estate, moving, gardens, horticulture, home maintenance. Send press releases to house and garden and home improvement magazines. Key words for search engine listings should include words that are related not only to gardening but also to home ownership and hobbies. Arrange "Most Beautiful Garden" contests on your site.

Qualifications needed: Designing skills. Gardening experience.

Educating yourself: Books, courses, working for a landscaping contractor for a few months.

Number of employees needed to start business (apart from yourself): 0

Things to watch out for: Business will tend to be slow during the winter months.

Additional income: Interior decorating consultant.

Find a similar business at: http://www.wwwcomm.com/flaggs

92. HOME IMPROVEMENT CENTER

Many professions are covered by the umbrella of home improvement: woodwork, siding, decks, flooring, carpentry, kitchens, bathrooms, painting/plastering, restoration, roofing, chimneys, windows, doors, extensions, wall covering and more. Almost every home owner indulges in a little bit of remodeling and construction from time to time, and most of them have no idea how to carry out their plans.

These home owners will find four important services in your site:

1. Consultation. The number of questions you will have to answer is infinite: where to find a certain tool, which tools to use, how to mix paint, where to get information on roofing, etcetera.

2. A virtual shop for basic tools and how-to books.

3. Free information. This is what visitors will come for in the first place, so you want this information to be as comprehensive as possible. Basic advice, FAQs, legal advice (e.g., permits), estimated costs, and comments from other visitors will be greatly appreciated by potential customers.

Start-up investment (other than Internet site costs and connection fees): $1,000-$50,000

International potential: None.

Special promotional strategies (in addition to those discussed in chapter 5): Establish links in sites that home owners are likely to visit: real estate businesses and information, home insurance, movers, lenders. Monitor related newsgroups (emphasize the free information on your site). Send press releases to hobby and craft, home and garden, regional and men's magazines.

Qualifications needed: A background in some of the home improvement professions is a plus.

Educating yourself: Literature, practice. Courses on video cassettes.

Number of employees needed to start business (apart from yourself): 0

Things to watch out for: Heavy, expensive tools may not sell well on the Internet. Concentrate on small tools, video cassettes and literature.

Additional income: Real estate database. Homeowners' insurance agency.

Find a similar business at: http://www.homeimprove.com/~plans

93. STEREO/HIGH FIDELITY EQUIPMENT CENTER

There is a fairly large community of people out there who consider themselves as stereophiles. Where ordinary people spend a couple of hundred of dollars on a portable CD or a basic stereo system, they spend a couple of thousands, and even tens of thousand of dollars on professional hi-grade equipment. This is an affluent group, and many of them are connected to the Internet.

You will not want to sell such expensive equipment on the Internet, since it is very unlikely that anyone would spend thousands of dollars on a sound system they could not even test. You can, however, concentrate on four services:

1. A referral service for local repair shops, dealers (new and used) and equipment rental outlets.

2. A part search service. Many of the parts these expensive systems use are very hard to come by, and especially in the case of old models. You will have to contact manufacturers, dealers, and jobbers (local and foreign) to find them.

3. Selling inexpensive equipment such as repair kits, headphones (some headphones are extremely expensive, though), and cables.

4. Selling literature: related reference books, courses in electronics and sound systems, etcetera.

In addition, don't forget to include some free information, such as FAQs, troubleshooting lists and even system reviews.

Start-up investment (other than Internet site costs and connection fees): $20,000-$100,000

International potential: Yes.

Special promotional strategies (in addition to those discussed in chapter 5): Send press releases to sound systems and music magazines. Establish links in sites that deal with electronics, sound systems and music (especially classical).

Qualifications needed: A background in electronics or sound systems is a plus.

Educating yourself: Books, courses, magazines and publications.

Number of employees needed to start business (apart from yourself): 0

Things to watch out for: Your potential customers are serious hobbyists or even professionals, so your site and the material found there must pass muster with them before they will consider returning to it, let alone use your services.

Additional income: A center for other high grade electronic equipment, such as video recorders and cameras, satellite dishes.

Find a similar business at: http://www.goodsound.com

94. ONLINE CONTRACTOR

Building your own house is not easy. It involves hiring many different contractors and experts, and working within a budget. Your business will be mainly a referral service for people who like to design and supervise the building of their own houses. Often, such people find themselves overwhelmed by the complexity and diversity of the task that lies ahead of them. They have to deal with contractors for: masonry, roofing, brickwork, bathrooms, kitchens, electrical works, plumbing, doors, windows, concrete, painting, siding and more.

Visitors to your site will be able, by entering their addresses in a special online form, to get a list of local contractors. In addition, you can:

➤ Refer your visitors to kit and prefab houses manufacturers.

➤ Sell plans and how-to books.

➤ Offer one on one consultation.

Don't forget to include as much free information and links as possible. Such information should deal mostly with contractors: how to find a good contractor, legal aspects, etcetera.

Start-up investment (other than Internet site costs and connection fees): $1,000-$20,000

International potential: None.

Special promotional strategies (in addition to those discussed in chapter 5): Send press releases to magazines that deal with real estate and construction. Emphasize the free features your site offers — FAQs, advice, referral service.

Qualifications needed: Some experience in working with contractors.

Educating yourself: Books, video cassettes, contacting local contractors.

Number of employees needed to start business (apart from yourself): 0

Things to watch out for: Make sure the contractors you refer your customers to are licensed and insured, and that they have a good record with the Better Business Bureau.

Additional income: Other referral services.

Find a similar business at: http://www.contractoronline.com

95. ONLINE CROSSWORD PUZZLES

With the huge variety of TV shows, computer games, movies and other forms of entertainment that are out there, it is remarkable that solving crossword puzzles has managed to remain a major pastime. Almost every newspaper features one, and crossword puzzle books, magazines and even computer games are still sold in the hundreds of millions throughout the world.

Your job will be either to create your own crossword puzzles, or take other people's puzzles (with their permission) and display them on your site. Your visitors will either print those puzzles directly from your site and solve them on paper (using a fax to send them over to you), or use special software they will find in your site to fill them in by using their computer keyboard. You will hold weekly contests where, following a drawing, a prize will be given to one of the people who solved the puzzles correctly. This strategy (so long as participation is free) will no doubt make your site a favorite among crossword puzzle lovers, and you will be able to capitalize on this popularity by:

1. Accepting advertising.

2. Selling crossword puzzle books, software, and magazines.

3. Help line: through e-mail, people will be able to ask for your help in solving difficult puzzles, finding missing key words, etcetera.

Start-up investment (other than Internet site costs and connection fees): $1,000-$20,000

International potential: Yes.

Special promotional strategies (in addition to those discussed in chapter 5): Send press releases to games and puzzles, and general interest magazines. Register your site with search engines under every key word that relates to pastime activities, games and entertainment.

Qualifications needed: None.

Educating yourself: Get a few good reference books.

Number of employees needed to start business (apart from yourself): 0

Things to watch out for: The prizes you give out must be big enough to attract people to your site, even if you don't anticipate a lot of visitors during the first months of operation. A book prize, for example, may not be enough to make someone take the time and trouble to solve a puzzle, but a hundred dollars or two might. Consult a lawyer about the prize drawing process.

Additional income: Other games and puzzles (e.g., jigsaw puzzles, riddles).

Find a similar business at: http://www.quizmaster.com/index.htm

96. ONLINE EDITOR

Often, people find themselves having to write an important letter, sales copy, brochure or leaflet. Word processors may be able to correct their spelling and very basic grammatical errors, but when it comes to more advanced grammar or style, they are at a loss. They can hire the services of a professional writer, of course, but this may take time, be very expensive, and at times very inconvenient.

The option your site will give them is to send the unedited text to you via e-mail (or fax, if they prefer to), entrusting you with making the necessary corrections, changes, and suggestions for better style. Offer two basic services (for short assignments): a low rate one to two business days service, and a more expensive expedited service that will probably be popular with business people who need to write a letter or a leaflet ASAP.

Your site can and should be very simple and small. A few lines about your business, skills and rates, one or two images, contact information, and that is about all. You can also allow visitors to key the text that needs editing into an online form, and for those without a laser printer you can offer typesetting/printing service.

Start-up investment (other than Internet site costs and connection fees): $1,000-$5,000

International potential: Yes. This service might be very popular with foreign business people who know some English and need to correspond with their English speaking counterparts.

Special promotional strategies (in addition to those discussed in chapter 5): Send press releases to business and trade magazines. Establish links in sites that offer services for businesses and that are visited by small business owners. Word of mouth is very important, so consider an introductory offer, such as editing the first business letter of any new customer for free.

Qualifications needed: Writing skills.

Educating yourself: Reference books, grammar and style books, educational software.

Number of employees needed to start business (apart from yourself): 0

Things to watch out for: Although some customers may take advantage of the free-first-letter-editing offer, it is still your best promotional tool, so don't drop it until you have more business than you can handle.

Additional income: Selling word processors, desktop publishers and reference books/software.

Find a similar business at: http://www.martinob.demon.co.uk

97. BUSINESS OPPORTUNITIES/JOB SEARCHER FOR SENIOR CITIZENS

Not everyone's idea of an ideal retirement is to sit in a rocking chair and count passing clouds all day. Not every retiree believes that he is well past his prime and is no longer able to work. Even more importantly, not every retiree can *afford* not to work. A huge number of retirees want to work, and are looking for part time jobs or businesses that don't require too many hours a day to operate.

But finding such a business or a job is very hard for a senior citizen, and his opportunities are extremely limited. Your site will help this ever growing group, who will find there:

1. A compilation of classified ads from local newspapers that offer part time jobs senior citizens can apply for.

2. Advice and information on self employment opportunities for senior citizens (e.g., car service driver).

3. Information on starting a business: FAQs, links, business ideas (pay phones, short delivery routes, tool sharpening), articles from other seniors, a referral service for lenders, addresses of relevant government agencies.

4. Consultation service. People who have never owned a business are likely to have many questions during the first few months of operation. Charge a nominal by-the-hour fee as most senior citizens are on a fixed budget.

5. User to user consultation service: match up senior citizens who are about to start their own business with other senior citizens who have some experience in that area and who are willing to share it with others.

6. A virtual shop for how-to books, software (for certain businesses), and lists of companies that work with home based assembly workers.

Start-up investment (other than Internet site costs and connection fees): $10,000-$50,000

International potential: None.

Special promotional strategies (in addition to those discussed in chapter 5): Send direct land mail to senior citizens' organizations and community centers. Send press releases to health and fitness, regional, and retirement magazines, and also to local newspapers.

Qualifications needed: None.

Educating yourself: You will need to subscribe to many local newspapers and to search online resources for job and business opportunities for the elderly. Acquaint yourself with business start-up procedures and with government agencies that help new businesses or senior citizens.

Number of employees needed to start business (apart from yourself): 0

Things to watch out for: Senior citizens rarely have sufficient funds for large investments, and some of them can afford only shoe-string enterprises. You have to be in tune with their special needs in order to provide the information and products they can really use. Welcome any comments they might have, and give them the opportunity to send them to you.

Additional income: An employment agency (for all ages).

Find a similar business at:
http://www.crm.mb.ca/crm/other/genmb/msch/msch10.html(non profit organization)

98. FOREIGN INVESTORS CENTER

Almost every country offers incentives for foreign investors (especially for industry), such as tax exempts, grants, low interest loans, free building lots, government participation in employee expenses, etcetera. Business people are always on the lookout for investment opportunities that will allow them to significantly reduce the cost of doing business. However, the task of contacting the multitude of consulates and commercial attachés and sorting out the information they need in order to make a decision and choose a country to invest in often has a daunting effect on these potential investors. Some business people are not even aware of the incentives foreign governments offer them.

Your site should list the incentives each country (including the U.S.) offers at present, plus an explanation of their meaning for the investor. Include a small search engine for your site. For example — the customer will select "government grants" and receive the list of all the countries that offer such grants to foreign investors.

Besides accepting advertising, you will derive your income from a referral service: any would-be investor would need lawyers and accountants to contact the foreign government of the country they want to invest in. Some of these lawyers/accountants/consultation services will have to be foreign based, which means that finding them (from another country) will not be easy. The service you provide by connecting the investor with them is therefore invaluable to him. You can also add a one-on-one consultation feature, where you will answer all the questions within your area of expertise, or you can sell books, information packages, or publications on the subject.

Start-up investment (other than Internet site costs and connection fees): $1,000-$10,000

International potential: Yes.

Special promotional strategies (in addition to those discussed in chapter 5): Establish links in sites that attract both local and foreign business people. Send press releases to business and trade magazines (including foreign magazines). Send direct land mail to trade organizations. When registering with search engines use key words that relate not only to investment and industry but also to grants, tax breaks, loans, government aid, etcetera.

Qualifications needed: A background in trade and accountancy will help you tremendously.

Educating yourself: Contact several different countries' consulates, and ask for material concerning foreign investments. Obtain foreign business directories (you can find them in the consulates' libraries) for lists of local lawyers, accountants, and other business services. Search online resources.

Number of employees needed to start business (apart from yourself): 0

Things to watch out for: Governments' policies change constantly. Make periodical checks to make sure the information on your site is up to date and accurate.

Additional income: Putting together consortiums of investors. Other services for businesses.

Find a similar business at: http://www.invloc.dk (a non profit organization)

99. ARMY NAVY CENTER

An army navy online center is more than just the online equivalent of an army navy store. This should be a center not just for collectors and military buffs, but also for new recruits and people who are considering joining the armed forces. Overall, your site should include:

1. Free information on armed forces recruitment, which will include links to armed forces information sites and addresses of

recruitment offices. Also of importance are FAQs, advice written by veterans and people in active service, information about benefits for recruits (e.g., college grants) and about army life.

2. One-on-one consultation. People about to join the armed forces have scores of questions that are sometimes best answered by someone who is not an official representative of the armed forces.

3. A virtual shop for books about preparing for basic training or on general military subjects. You can also sell equipment new recruits need during basic training, such as sewing kits, small flashlights, pocket-size electric shavers.

4. A virtual army navy shop — uniforms, bandages, snaplights, utensil sets, boots, canteens, camping gear, knapsacks, and any memorabilia or surplus goods that will appeal to collectors.

Start-up investment (other than Internet site costs and connection fees): $20,000-$100,000

International potential: Yes (for selling memorabilia).

Special promotional strategies (in addition to those discussed in chapter 5): Establish links in sites that appeal to young people, students, and collectors. Send press releases to career, entertainment, and military magazines. You may also want to contact editors of high school newspapers. Monitor related newsgroups.

Qualifications needed: None, but prior military service is a definite plus.

Educating yourself: Books, publications, contacting government agencies, collectors' catalogs (of military memorabilia).

Number of employees needed to start business (apart from

yourself): 0

Things to watch out for: Some military surplus items are available only in large quantities. Avoid investing too heavily in an item that you are not certain you can sell in large quantities, even if it means passing up a great deal.

Additional income: Selling camping equipment and books.

Find a similar business at:
http://www.colbubbie.com/

100. CUSTOM FRAMES

This site can be created as an interactive virtual shop that will appeal even to people who are not interested in buying frames. Custom frames are needed for every photograph or painting that does not fall within the standard frame sizes (3½x5, 4x6, 5x7, 8x10, 11x14). To order them, people usually have to go to a custom frame shop, choose a certain design and size, and wait for the order to be ready for pickup. You can do all this on your site. The customer will be able to choose from a selection of dozens of frame types and colors, and then enter the desired size and any special requirement (e.g., a mat inside the frame) she might have. The custom-designed frame will then come to life online (without the picture in it, of course) and the customer will be able to view the finished frame in the right proportions (and preferably in 3D). If the customer is satisfied with the result, the order will go through and payment will be taken. If not, she will go back to the designing page and start over.

You can assemble the frames yourself or work with a sub contractor. Another service you can provide is inserting the picture (which the customer will send to you) into the finished frame and sending the customer the completed product.

Start-up investment (other than Internet site costs and connection fees): $10,000-$50,000

International potential: Yes.

Special promotional strategies (in addition to those discussed in chapter 5): Send press releases to photography, art, house and garden and home improvement magazines. Establish links in sites that deal with those subjects as well as decorating, hobbies, family trees, nostalgia, crafts, and gifts.

Qualifications needed: None.

Educating yourself: Visit custom frame shops and find out from them (not from the manufacturers) which frame styles are the most popular. The manufacturer you work with may be honest, but bear in mind that some frame manufacturers will try to unload the designs they are stuck with on the retailer. For you it will only be a waste of site space, and it will make your selection less attractive.

Number of employees needed to start business (apart from yourself): 0

Things to watch out for: Creating this site (especially with the 3D option) might prove expensive. However, it is necessary in order to stand out from the crowd.

Additional income: Selling photo related items: films (by the brick), albums, ready made standard-size frames, simple cameras.

Find a similar business at: http://www.awcframes.com

101. SMALL BUSINESSES CENTER

This service will concentrate under one site all the information small business owners and entrepreneurs about to open such businesses need to know: which forms to fill, which is the best business entity to apply for (corporation, limited partnership), how to apply for loans and government aid, where to find free government and tax consultation services, which licenses are required and more. Visitors to your site should also be able to find links to related sites, business services, and government offices.

The commercial part of your site can include:

1. Information packages — either in the form of leaflets or e-mail messages — concerning tax issues, business plans, marketing, etcetera.

2. A referral service for lawyers, CPAs, special consultants.

3. A virtual shop for forms, books, office supplies, software.

Start-up investment (other than Internet site costs and connection fees and fees): $5,000-$50,000

International potential: None.

Special promotional strategies (in addition to those discussed in chapter 5): Send press releases to business and finance, and regional magazines. Key words for search engines should include (in addition to words referring to small business issues): job, retirement, investment, money, income, unemployment, layoff.

Qualifications needed: Having owned and operated a business is a minimum requirement.

Educating yourself: Books, courses, tax workshops, consultation (some is provided free of charge by government agencies) and official publications.

Number of employees needed to start business (apart from yourself): 0

Things to watch out for: In order to create repeat visitors, make sure the information on your site is updated frequently, and add new features and services from time to time.

Additional income: A service that deals with business closure, insolvency and bankruptcy. An incorporation service.

Find a similar business at: http://www.thevine.com

102. MOTORCYCLE CENTER

Motorcyclists say that their real expenses begin *after* the purchase of the bike itself. The variety of accessories and protective devices for motorcyclists is enormous. Unlike car owners, for whom accessories are an option, motorcyclists *must* buy at least some of them (helmets, gloves). The longer they keep the bike, the more riding gear and accessories they will buy. Even before the advent of the Internet, many, if not most, of these items were sold through catalogs, and so buying from an online catalog will be a very natural step for a motorcyclist.

To appeal to your potential customers, your site must also include free information: riding tips, how to find low-rate insurance, FAQs, model info, performance data, technical advice, links to related sites. Also — dedicate a space in your site for visitors' own articles and comments. You can even arrange these by subject. For example, the visitor will select "ZX-9" from the menu, and will be shown any comments about this motorcycle that other visitors have posted.

Your income will be derived from:

1. A referral service for: repair shops, advanced riding schools, racing schools, new and used motorcycle dealers.

2. A virtual catalog. You can include any item that appears in conventional catalogs: protective gear, tires, covers, gloves, repair kits, lubricants, engine parts, etcetera. You can stock the items yourself, which will be very expensive, or work on a drop-ship basis with another dealer or with different manufacturers.

3. Selling literature: owners' manuals, service manuals, riding guides, used bike guides. You can also include video cassettes (e.g., of racing events, riding lessons, etc.).

Start-up investment (other than Internet site costs and connection fees): $1,000-$100,000

International potential: Yes (some countries impose limitations on the import of certain parts, though).

Special promotional strategies (in addition to those discussed in chapter 5): Establish links in sites that deal with transportation, sports, hobbies and outdoor activities. Send press releases to motorcycle magazines. You can contact riding schools directly and offer them a free listing in your site's referral service in exchange for giving your Internet address to students.

Qualifications needed: None.

Educating yourself: Magazines, books. Contact catalog companies.

Number of employees needed to start business (apart from yourself): 0

Things to watch out for: Make sure your delivery time (or the delivery time of the dealer you work with) is short, and that the items you offer are of high quality. Motorcyclists tend to be more selective than car owners about the products they buy. Your site will have to be large and a little expensive to maintain in order to include the hundreds of photographs needed for your online catalog.

Additional income: A boating center.

Find a similar business at: http://www.accwhse.com

103. VIRTUAL CEMETERY

Your job will be to help people perpetuate the memory of their deceased loved ones by allowing them to erect virtual tombs on your site. For an annual fee, a space in your site will be rented where a picture of the deceased, together with a few lines written by the mourners, will be posted. The virtual tomb can also include audio and video files, and even links to other sites or virtual tombs. Family and friends of the deceased will thus be able to hear his voice, see video clips, view pictures, go to sites that were of interest to him, or visit virtual tombs of other family members. For an additional fee, a customer will be able to display a small memorial plaque on your site's home page for a predetermined period of time (a day, a week). Another source of income for you will be offering your services in designing the virtual tombs, or even writing their content.

A possible addition to this service is a virtual pet cemetery. The two sites can be intertwined or completely separated and independent from one another. As the subject matter is lighter, a pet virtual cemetery can come with special effects, such as background sounds (e.g., barking) that will start playing automatically whenever the virtual tomb is visited.

Start-up investment (other than Internet site costs and connection fees): $1,000-$5,000

International potential: Yes.

Special promotional strategies (in addition to those discussed in chapter 5): This is a service of general appeal; no need to concentrate on any specific target group (sending direct mail to families of recently deceased people should be regarded as highly inappropriate). Consider offering a one-month-trial-period for new customers.

Qualifications needed: None.

Number of employees needed to start business (apart from yourself): 0

Things to watch out for: This site should look dignified and respectful of the dead. Among other things, this means that you will not be able to accept advertising on your site, and that you will not be able to use hyped-up sales copy.

Additional income: Religious goods center.

Find a similar business at: http://www.worldgardens.com

104. CRISIS AND DEPRESSION CENTER

When a disaster strikes, or when people are overcome by dangerous and debilitating depression, they often don't know where to turn to for help. Hot lines for people who suffer from depression or panic exist throughout the world, but most people who undergo a crisis ignore them because they are viewed as last resorts for suicidal cases; something which leaves the caller with a stigma.

A crisis and depression center is not a hot line (although it is a good idea to display hot line telephone numbers on your site). It is an online service that aims to help people in need by showing them the right course of action. Your site can include:

1. A virtual shop for literature and informative video/audio cassettes. Sell any book, audio or video cassette that deals with the mental aspects of crises, the dangers of depression, and other psychological and self-help issues.

2. Links to sites that specialize in psychological issues or self help.

3. A referral service for local clinics and therapists.

4. Free information: articles written by professionals or depression victims who share their stories, FAQs.

5. One on one consultation service through e-mail or chat/Internet telephony programs.

Start-up investment (other than Internet site costs and connection fees): $20,000-$30,000

International potential: Yes.

Special promotional strategies (in addition to those discussed in chapter 5): Links to and from sites that deal with psychological and self help issues, and also sites that deal with psychic services (to which distressed people sometimes turn). Send press releases to magazines that deal with the above issues, and also to general interest or regional magazines.

Qualifications needed: If you offer a one-on-one consultation service, a license may be required.

Educating yourself: Books, magazines, publications, interviews with professionals, courses, seminars, university education.

Number of employees needed to start business (apart from yourself): 0

Things to watch out for: This online service is no substitute for professional help; if you recognize (through one on one consultation) that you are dealing with a suicidal person, refer that person to the appropriate professional help, or even notify the authorities yourself.

Additional income: Sites dedicated to self bettering, family matters, relationship problems.

Find a similar business at: http://www.siec.ca

105. CLIPPING SERVICE

Manufacturers, retailers, and service companies are always looking for ways to monitor their publicity. Finding every mention of themselves or their products in various newspapers is a time consuming task that most companies cannot afford to perform themselves. What they do instead is hire a clipping service, whose job it is to record any mention of the company name or product throughout hundreds of magazines and newspapers, both online and paper based. Other potential customers are rival companies or just about anyone who is looking for material on a certain company, product or even an individual executive.

A specific service you can provide will be to find book reviews in online and paper-based magazines. Writers, publishers, and literary agents rarely have the time to do this themselves, and will greatly appreciate your service.

You will have to spend a considerable amount of time going through hundreds of magazines and online resources and creating a database. The key to success in this business is the ability to scan an article in a magazine and quickly pick out one or two key words (usually the company or person's name) for use with your reference list. Once this list is put together, searching for a specific company, product or person will take minutes. A computer is a must for this type of business.

Start-up investment (other than Internet site costs and connection fees): $5,000-$15,000

International potential: Yes.

Special promotional strategies (in addition to those discussed in

chapter 5): Establish links in sites that offer services for businesses, or that deal with promotion, advertising, and media. List your business with search engines not only as a clipping service but also as a database (limited to magazine articles). Send press releases to trade, consumer, and business magazines.

Qualifications needed: None.

Educating yourself: Directories, publications and magazines.

Number of employees needed to start business (apart from yourself): 0

Things to watch out for: Subscription to hundreds of magazines and newspapers will be costly. You will have to begin compiling a reference list a few months before you start your business.

Additional income: Online search service.

Find a similar business at: http://www.teleclip.com

106. INTERNET ACCESS FOR PEOPLE WITH DISABILITIES CENTER

With the special software and hardware available today to help disabled people work with computers, there is no reason why any disabled person should not take an active part in the online world. Unfortunately, many disabled people are not aware of this. They do not have computers and consequently have little to do with the Internet. Sadder still is the fact that it is exactly this particular group, who due to their disabilities suffer from communication problems with the outside world (and often from isolation), who would benefit the most from the new world the Internet can open for them.

Unlike most businesses in this book, this site appeals not to the potential customers themselves (they do not yet have Internet access), but to their friends, relatives, associates, and care-takers. Through them, you will get your message across to the disabled person: you *can* join the online world!

Your site will list the special methods used by disabled people to work with computers and with the Internet. These methods will be displayed according to the disability. If the person is visually impaired, he can use screen readers (a software that reads the text off the screen) or Braille devices (which work in quite the same way, but with special hardware attached to the computer). A person who is physically impaired can use special keyboards (enlarged keyboards, keyboards with keyguards), a single-switch control (e.g., for people who can move only their heads), or voice input devices. Special software and hardware also exist to help disabled people work with specific platforms, such as Windows or Macintosh.

You can derive your income either from selling the software and hardware directly to the customer, or by operating a referral or drop ship service in agreement with the manufacturers. Free information on your site can include FAQs, links and product information.

Start-up investment (other than Internet site costs and connection fees): $1,000-$100,000

International potential: Yes.

Special promotional strategies (in addition to those discussed in chapter 5): Send direct land mail to people with disabilities associations, organizations, clinics, community centers. Issue press releases to health and disability magazines. Establish links in sites that deal with similar issues and general Internet issues.

Qualifications needed: None.

Educating yourself: Business directories. Contact manufacturers of the special software and hardware you are going to sell.

Number of employees needed to start business (apart from

yourself): 0

Things to watch out for: Keep yourself up to date on this industry. It sometimes seems that new software and innovations in this field are introduced almost daily.

Additional income: A virtual shop for conventional items for disabled people. A referral service for businesses that deal with home remodeling for disabled people.

Find a similar business at: http://bucky.aa.uic.edu (non profit organization).

107. LINK CENTER

This is one of the simplest online businesses to operate. You need to pick a subject matter (for example: fishing) and designate your site as a link page to sites that deal with that subject. As a result, every user interested in your site's subject matter will make it first on his list because every site and online point of interest that deals with his favorite subject can be reached from there. Your site will become a menu, a master directory of that particular subject. You can make it either in the form of a Gopher or a Web site, and in addition to the links you can add:

1. Free information and FAQs about the subject matter.

2. A search engine/database to help users narrow down their search. In the case of the subject matter being fishing, the user may want to limit his search to "trout".

3. A "Contact-Us" section that will allow users to ask questions, offer their contributions (e.g., new links they have found), etcetera.

4. A "What's-New" feature that will tell users of any new sites that

were added to the list of links recently.

In theory, your income can be derived from a referral fee that you will charge the sites you link to. While this may be a good idea for some businesses, the overall effect will be a decrease in the number of links, and consequently, in the depth of coverage your site offers. Instead, you should base your income on:

➤ Advertising fees.

➤ A virtual shop that will sell related items or information (according to your site's subject matter).

Start-up investment (other than Internet site costs and connection fees): $1,000-$100,000

International potential: Yes.

Special promotional strategies (in addition to those discussed in chapter 5): Register your site with search engines under any key word that relates to its subject matter. In essence, your entire promotion will have to be shaped by your site's subject matter.

Qualifications needed: None.

Educating yourself: Spending many hours surfing Internet sites and online resources.

Number of employees needed to start business (apart from yourself): 0

Things to watch out for: Make sure that your virtual shop appears only as a link on your site. Remember: your main feature is links. If the shop takes over the site and becomes the main feature, the non-commercial, free-public-service attitude that would have attracted users will not be there. You can, however, promote your virtual shop by displaying an advertisement for it on your site.

Additional income: An online promotion service that will help new sites establish their links in appropriate sites.

Find a similar business at: http://www.baseball-links.com

108. PRESS RELEASE SERVICE

Magazine editors usually print the press releases submitted to them "as-is", and at any rate, the only alteration you should expect of them will be to shorten your press release. For this reason, the way your press release is presented to the public is very much dependent on your own writing skills.

But not everyone can produce a convincing, professional-looking press release that would sweep readers off their feet or at least make them take notice of the company or product mentioned there. This is where the professional press release writer comes in.

There are many types of press releases: for Internet sites, for books, for products, for services, for new business entities, etcetera. You can, of course, write the press release and send it to the customer via e-mail, but to make this a complete press release service, it is better to send it directly to the newspapers, magazines, and any other media upon which you have agreed with your customer. In addition to your main service, you can offer consultation services and help customers find the right magazines or newspapers for their press release.

An important aspect of your business will be the "personal touch" approach. Editors are often tired of receiving introduction letters (attached to the press releases) that look like mass-produced form letters. While editors do realize that your press release must have been sent to other newspapers as well, they don't like to receive junk mail. A personal touch approach will make the accompanying letters seem more personal, and will make the recipient feel that the writer had that particular magazine in mind when he wrote the letter.

Start-up investment (other than Internet site costs and connection

fees): $1,000-$5,000

International potential: Yes.

Special promotional strategies (in addition to those discussed in chapter 5): Send press releases to trade and business magazines. Establish links in sites that deal with services for businesses and especially with advertising and promotion. Show convincing samples of your work on your site.

Qualifications needed: None.

Educating yourself: Hone your writing skills. Read as many press releases as possible and save a few copies of the best of them for future references (for more information, see pages 76-80).

Number of employees needed to start business (apart from yourself): 0

Things to watch out for: You may need to get a fax in order to allow businesses who do not have a scanner to send you material (e.g., brochures) about themselves and their product. Make sure you get your customers' approval of the finished press release in writing before submitting it to the appropriate magazines.

Additional income: A virtual shop for books about promotion, marketing, selling, and advertising.

Find a similar business at:
http://patriot.net/~bmcgin/pressrel.html

109. ONLINE WAKE UP SERVICE

Telephone wake-up services have been around for decades. It is an ideal online business that involves no merchandise, no land delivery, and very little work on the entrepreneur's behalf.
Your site can be small and simple. It should be equipped with an online

form that will enable customers to key in the data needed to carry out this service. The customer will need to spend only a few moments in your site, leaving her personal information and taking care of payment. You can either charge your customers via credit cards or e-cash, or, because of the small amounts involved (probably no more than two dollars per call), you can set up a BBS with a 900 number. A monthly fee (entitling the customer to a predetermined number of calls within one month) might also be a good idea for some customers. Long distance calls (within the continental U.S.) rarely cost more than 25 cents for the first (and, in the case of a wake-up call, last) minute even during standard time, so the potential profit is high.

Start-up investment (other than Internet site costs and connection fees): $1,000-$20,000

International potential: Limited (high international calling rates will force you to raise your prices).

Special promotional strategies (in addition to those discussed in chapter 5): Establish links in sites that offer services for businesses, or that attract business people and professionals. Send press releases to business and trade magazines. Offer introductory deals such as a second wake-up call for free.

Qualifications needed: None.

Educating yourself: Study the market in order to determine the optimal fee to charge for your service.

Number of employees needed to start business (apart from yourself): 0

Things to watch out for: Automated dialing equipment is costly. You may want to make the wake-up calls manually until the amount of business you get justifies such an investment.

Additional income: A reminder service.

Find a similar business at:
http://www.alphabase.com/ten//teninfo.html

110. ONLINE CARTOONIST

Who uses cartoons and comic strips? Well, newspapers, of course; but also corporations who need them for their advertising campaigns, various institutes and organizations who use them to enhance educational material, software creators, advertising agencies, government agencies, and home page/Web site creators, whose number is increasing daily. Other potential customers are online magazines, whose number is also steadily growing and who strive to make their text-based publications more graphically appealing.

The Internet is the perfect medium for this art form. You can display samples of your work on your site, or even include a complete image bank for customers to select from. Cartoons can be downloaded instantaneously, printed directly from your site, or sent by mail to the buyer. Through e-mail and Internet telephony you can also receive instructions for made-by-order cartoons. In order to secure such jobs it is important to include in your site samples that will convince potential customers of your talent and abilities.

Start-up investment (other than Internet site costs and connection fees): $1,000-$5,000

International potential: Yes.

Special promotional strategies (in addition to those discussed in chapter 5): Invite Internet users (even those who are not potential customers) to see the cartoons in your site. Making your site an ongoing online exhibition will ensure that an increasing number of people will hear of it through word of mouth. Feature "a comic strip of the day" on your home page. Send press releases to trade and business magazines. Establish links in sites that appeal to business people. Send direct land mail to newspapers and magazines (don't forget small regional magazines).

Qualifications needed: Drawing skills and imagination.

Educating yourself: Cartoon drawing can be learned from books, courses, and even software. Search directories such as *Writer's Market* for listings of magazines and other publications that might be interested in your work.

Number of employees needed to start business (apart from yourself): 0

Things to watch out for: This is a highly competitive business. Success will not come overnight.

Additional income: A virtual shop for comic books, comic strip collections, how-to (draw cartoons) books, etcetera.

Find a similar business at:
http://ww4.choice.net/~ktbarney/thenose/index.html

111. ONLINE HUMOR/JOKE WRITER

In their efforts to spruce up a speech or lighten up a businesslike public speaking occasion, corporate executives often rely on humor. However, not everyone has the gift of laughter or the time to think of jokes to add to their speeches, and most business executives will greatly appreciate a service such as this.

Your potential customer will send you (by e-mail or fax) the text of the speech or even just the gist of it. You will add the humorous parts where you believe they are necessary, and send the work back to the customer. Aside from speeches, your service can also cover leaflets, brochures, and just about any communicative piece in need of livening up.

To convince visitors of your talent, your site must display the best samples of your work and (with time) a list of satisfied customers and their comments on your service. Even more important are credentials: past experience, clubs or shows you appeared on, newspaper articles you have written, famous comedians you have written material for, etcetera.

In addition to corporate work — your bread and butter — you can of course write freelance material for online and conventional newspapers as well as radio and TV shows.

Start-up investment (other than Internet site costs and connection fees): $1,000-$5,000

International potential: Yes (this is an especially useful service for foreign business people who are about to address English speaking crowds).

Special promotional strategies (in addition to those discussed in chapter 5): Establish links in sites that deal with services for businesses and that attract executives. Send press releases to trade and business magazines. Include audio files of your material in your site and invite visitors to listen to a free "10 minutes of comedy."

Qualifications needed: A knack for tickling people's funny bone.

Educating yourself: Listen to and read as much comedy material as possible, but try to develop your own distinctive trademark style.

Number of employees needed to start business (apart from yourself): 0

Things to watch out for: Don't forget for a moment that your job is only to mollify the effect of a speech or to lighten it up, and never to take over, change its meaning, or insult its listeners. Entertaining the crowd is not the main purpose of the executive who has written this speech.

Additional income: Online speech writer. Public speaking consultant.

Find a similar business at: http://www.jokenet.com

112. ONLINE COMPOSER

We sometimes come to think of the Internet as a kind of a virtual book; as a collection of texts and graphics. In fact, the Internet is a multimedia tool. It can allow the user access to audio and even video files, and in essence it encompasses all the features of books, radio, television, PC's, and even the telephone. For composers, who until now were quite limited in displaying their products to the public, the Internet is therefore a heavensent tool.

As an online composer, samples of your work will be displayed on your site as audio files (such as Realaudio) that users can click on and hear the content of. You don't have to compose the pieces yourself, of course. There are thousands of young aspiring musicians who are waiting to be discovered and who will be more than happy to work with you on a consignment basis. If you or the composer you work with have any background in radio, TV, or the music industry, don't forget to mention this on your site.

Who will your clients be? Advertising agencies, hotels, software creators, amateur theatrical groups, strip malls, and other retailers who want to play their own jingles in their establishments. Also, many people today enhance their sites by adding background music that plays automatically whenever a user reaches the home page. You can sell them both the music and the information on how to set up the auto-player. Musical pieces can be sent to your customers on cassettes, floppy disks, CD's or as downloadable files. Through e-mail/Internet telephony, your clients can also contact the composer and request a musical piece to be written according to their instructions.

Start-up investment (other than Internet site costs and connection fees): $1,000-$5,000

International potential: Yes.

Special promotional strategies (in addition to those discussed in chapter 5): Establish links in sites that appeal to online entrepreneurs and business people. Send direct land mail to advertising agencies and software developers. Issue press releases to regional, online, and retail business magazines. Your site should appeal to all Internet users, not just to potential customers — word of mouth is the key to your success.

Qualifications needed: Being a talented musician or having the knack for finding one.

Educating yourself: Familiarize yourself with the music industry — contracts, royalties, licensing, etcetera.

Number of employees needed to start business (apart from yourself): 0

Things to watch out for: This is a highly competitive business. Unless you (or the composer you represent) are an established musician, don't expect to make a living out of this business during the first year of operation. You may want to consult a lawyer before drafting the contracts for the musicians you represent.

Additional income: Online music lessons. A virtual music shop (CD's, notes, accessories for musical instruments).

Find a similar business at: http://www.circusmusic.com

113. CUSTOMIZED CHECKS

Any mail-order business would usually make a good online business, and customized check printers have long relied on mail-orders to generate a major part of their income.

Your site should look very much like the mail-order catalogs you have probably received more than once from customized check printers. It should display the various check designs you have, prices, and delivery options. Try to develop your own unique line — don't just rely on the same old ideas mail order check printers or banks use. However, be sensitive to the laws of supply and demand; a check design will not be popular just because it is original. It will probably be a good idea to let customers contact you through e-mail and send you their comments and suggestions for the designs displayed on your site.

You can also allow your customers to custom-design their own checks: for an additional fee, the customers will send you a picture that they want to appear on their checks, and you will print it according to their instructions. Don't confuse this service with printing personalized checks: the customer's name and address will have to be printed on all orders for no extra charge (in addition, of course, to account and routing numbers).

Start-up investment (other than Internet site costs and connection fees): $10,000-$50,000

International potential: Yes (if banking regulations in your foreign client's country permit this).

Special promotional strategies (in addition to those discussed in chapter 5): This service is of a general appeal, and should not be aimed at one group in particular. Establish links in high-traffic sites. If you want to send press releases, think of a unique (and perhaps free) service you can offer on your site in order to interest editors. Consider paying royalties to creators of popular figures (e.g., cartoons) to use them with your designs.

Qualifications needed: None.

Educating yourself: Study the selections of customized check printers. Learn which designs are fashionable or "in".

Number of employees needed to start business (apart from yourself): 0

Things to watch out for: Add new designs constantly, and replace those that are not in demand. Capitalize on popular trends (TV or screen figures, political statements), and remember that some of the most popular check designs are banal, corny and boring.

Additional income: Greeting cards. Address labels.

Find a similar business at: http://www.hotnew.com/checks

114. ONLINE BOOKSTORE

In many of the business ideas covered in this book there is a mention of selling (related) books as one of the additional sources of income. Books are the most widely purchased item on the Internet. An online bookstore is therefore one of the best online businesses you can start. You can make it an extension of an existing conventional bookstore, or a business in its own right. Bookstores usually enjoy better credit terms from wholesalers/distributors than most stores get from their suppliers, and the return policy is also more flexible. In a nut shell, as long as the books were not damaged in the store itself, you virtually (though not officially) have a consignment arrangement with the distributors. If you don't want to buy the books or you are strapped for cash, you can work on a drop-ship basis with established mail order/online bookstores or even with a local bookstore.

Although nothing is stopping you from opening a general interest bookstore, you are probably better off starting a more limited, specialized store. Your business will appear more serious, and it will help you to attract customers (who are likely to visit a bookstore that deals with the subject they are interested in) and to cut down on start up costs. Specialized bookstores can be dedicated to: how-to books, mystery, history books, textbooks, literary works, ethnic books, biographies and more.

Other than listing the books you have for sale, you would also want to allow your customers access to an on-site database (for example, to enable them to look up the name of a certain author), reviews (for some of the books), readers' comments, and even excerpts from a few books (these can be in the form of text based articles or even audio excerpts read by a narrator).

Start-up investment (other than Internet site costs and connection fees): $1,000-$100,000

International potential: Yes.

Special promotional strategies (in addition to those discussed in chapter 5): Establish links in sites that deal with the subject matter of your books. Contact publishers and offer to participate in direct advertising: you will share their mailing expenses, and they will advertise your site on the brochures they send to their mailing list. Don't spend too much on such advertisement though — not everyone on the publishers' mailing lists has Internet access.

Qualifications needed: None.

Educating yourself: Visit bookstores, view best seller lists, read book reviews. Shop around for the distributors and jobbers that will give you the best credit terms.

Number of employees needed to start business (apart from yourself): 0-1

Things to watch out for: Some distributors may not be too happy to work with an online-only bookstore. You may want to play down this aspect of your business when you first contact them. You will probably need a storage space for the books.

Additional income: Selling books-on-tape, CD-ROM books, software.

Find a similar business at: http://www.amazon.com

115. NATURE ONLINE

The more we allow technology to take over our lives and the more we find ourselves cocooned in our urban environments, the more we want to rediscover nature. Nature TV shows are as popular as they have ever been, environmentalism is on the rise, and exotic pets are no longer a rarity in modern cities.

Your site can give your visitors:

1. Links to sites that deal with the animal world, reservations, special societies and organizations, tourism, etcetera.

2. A referral service for travel agencies that deal with exotic/nature trips (e.g., to the rain forests, safaris).

3. A virtual shop for books, video cassettes, CD-ROMs, posters, gifts (such as animal figures and souvenirs). This is your main source of income.

4. Free information: statistics, databases, exotic pets, where and how to volunteer for conservation/research projects, etcetera.

5. Photographs and artwork, audio files (sounds of nature). This should be a constantly changing exhibition to ensure repeat visitors.

6. Visitors' contributions: articles, stories, pictures.

7. Children's center: games, interactive visual and audio displays,

information, links.

8. Related job opportunities. Anything from a pet shop assistant to a cook for an arctic expedition.

Start-up investment (other than Internet site costs and connection fees): $10,000-$50,000

International potential: Yes.

Special promotional strategies (in addition to those discussed in chapter 5): Establish links in sites that deal with tourism, the animal and plant worlds, pets. Send press releases to animal, nature, ecology, and travel/camping magazines. Consider holding a quiz or a contest (such as best wild animal photograph) on your site.

Qualifications needed: None.

Educating yourself: Publications, books, clip art/stock photography catalogs. Join related organizations.

Number of employees needed to start business (apart from yourself): 0

Things to watch out for: This site requires constant updating and changing in order to maintain a solid customer base.

Additional income: A pet center.

Find a similar business at: http://www.discovery.com/

116. PUBLISHING BOOKS ONLINE

If you have ever seen a CD-ROM book, you probably know that publishing a book on CD-ROM means a lot more than just putting text into it. CD-ROM books are interactive and full of pictures, graphics, audio and even video files. The same concept can be transferred to the Web.

For example, let's assume that you want to publish a children's book online. Each Web page of the online book will have text and illustrations, along with audio or video files. The illustrations can be interactive. For example, clicking on the door of a house will take the user to a picture of the living room (on another Web page); clicking on a picture of a dog will produce barking sounds. At the bottom of every page "forward" and "back" buttons will allow the visitor to browse the online book as they please.

Although children's books, short and full of pictures, are probably the best choice for online publishing, there are also many adult books that you can transfer to this medium: short how-to books with sketches, directories, travel books with maps and pictures, and even short fiction. Your site should be free, and your income will be derived from:

1. Accepting advertising.

2. Promoting the sale of CD-ROM books, especially more books in the same series as the online book ("If you want to read more of the adventures of.... order the next book in the.... series"). Of course, you can also promote the sale of conventional books, or open a virtual bookstore.

3. Personalizing a book. Parents will order a short CD-ROM book that features their children as the heros. This can be done by simply changing the names in the book's text, or, for an additional fee, also by including a few pictures of the child in the book.

Start-up investment (other than Internet site costs and connection fees): $10,000-$50,000

International potential: Yes.

Special promotional strategies (in addition to those discussed in chapter 5): As long as entering the site is free, this is the kind of business that will promote itself. It will probably interest What's-New services, so let them know of your site's existence. Send press releases to magazines that deal with the subject of your books, and also to entertainment, family and literary magazines.

Qualifications needed: None.

Educating yourself: Purchase a few CD-ROM books and study them. Take courses or read literature about operating the software you need for creating your online or CD-ROM books. Contact aspiring young artists for illustrations, and struggling actors for recording the audio files of the book.

Number of employees needed to start business (apart from yourself): 0

Things to watch out for: Since Web pages download a lot slower than pages on a CD-ROM book, there are some limitations you must consider. You have to allow for reasonable downloading time, and this means medium to small illustrations, plain backgrounds, short audio files, text only option (for adult books), and a limited amount of gimmicks. Overall, don't make your online books too long.

Additional income: Selling toys and games (if you publish an online children's book). Publishing online courses.

Find a similar business at:
http://www.obs-us.com/chesler/ne/06/jump.htm

117. PILOT TRAINING/PLANE OWNERS CENTER

People who want to become pilots spend a lot of money on the process. Aircraft owners spend even more. There is no reason why at least some of this money should not reach its destination through online services. Aircraft owners and many pilots have higher than average incomes, and are technically inclined. They are therefore highly likely to have Internet access.

The most common pilot license is that of a "private pilot" class, and most of the material in your site will have to deal with it. There is also a more limited "recreational pilot" class, as well as instrument rating and commercial classes, which are much more difficult and demand a serious commitment in time and money.

Visitors to your site should find:

1. Free information: licensing requirements, insurance problems, FAQs, reviews of new navigation & communication equipment, safety tips, advice from veteran pilots and instructors, mechanical troubleshooting charts.

2. A referral service for flying schools, aviation career academies, airframe and powerplant mechanics, technicians, insurance companies, kit manufacturers, loan brokers, replacement parts manufacturers.

3. Classifieds: career opportunities in aviation, aircrafts and equipment for sale, ultralight aircrafts, business opportunities.

4. A virtual store for: Video/CD-ROM courses, literature, maps and charts, software (especially simulators), inexpensive equipment and pilot supplies.

5. Links to similar sites (e.g., relevant associations and organizations, online aviation magazines).

Start-up investment (other than Internet site costs and connection fees): $10,000-$100,000

International potential: Limited (licensing requirements vary from country to country).

Special promotional strategies (in addition to those discussed in chapter 5): Issue press releases to aviation magazines. Send direct land mail to aviation organizations and associations.

Qualifications needed: A background in aviation is a definite plus.

Educating yourself: Courses, magazines, video cassettes, flight instruction, business directories.

Number of employees needed to start business (apart from yourself): 0

Things to watch out for: Since there are about ten wannabe pilots for every licensed pilot, you may want to address that group as well, and sell popular aviation literature (e.g., about military aircraft) in addition to professional, technical material. You can also sell aircraft jewelry and model kits.

Additional income: Marine center: motorboats, sailboats, supplies and accessories and so on.

Find a similar business at: http://www.globalair.com

118. WOOD PRODUCTS

In an age when technology surrounds us with cold, mass produced products made of plastic and metal, more and more people have grown to appreciate pristine hand-made wood products.

The wood products you will make will have to be small enough to send by mail or other inexpensive delivery methods. Such products can include: shelves, (collapsible) birdhouses, flower boxes, cases, nut-crackers, book holders, and many other useful items. You will need to set aside a room in your house (preferably the garage) for woodworking, and purchase the right tools. The mark up is very high, and your only major investment will be in tools.

You should display high quality pictures of your products on your site together with pricing information and available finishing options (e.g., the item's color). Many of your customers will probably buy your products as gifts, so you may want to provide them with greeting cards and special wrapping options. If you don't have the time or the expertise, you should consider buying some of your items from outside sources. This is especially practical for statues, figures, decorations and other delicate works of art.

Start-up investment (other than Internet site costs and connection fees): $10,000-$30,000

International potential: Limited to small, light weight items.

Special promotional strategies (in addition to those discussed in chapter 5): Establish links in sites that deal with gifts, holidays, nature, hobbies and craft. Register your site in search engines under words relating to these subjects as well as wood products.

Qualifications needed: None.

Educating yourself: Books, videos, practice. Search department stores and gift catalogs for new ideas.

Number of employees needed to start business (apart from yourself): 0

Things to watch out for: Get a professional photographer to take the products' pictures. The importance of having a high quality picture of the (high quality) products cannot be stressed enough — this is the thing that will make or break your business. Make sure your prices are not set too low, and that visitors are aware of the fact that your products were not mass produced by a large manufacturer.

Additional income: Selling woodworking tools, instructional videos and literature, and plans. Chainsaw sculpting.

Find a similar business at:
http://www.agentz.com/qwp/index.html

119. MUSIC CENTER

Music items are among the most widely purchased items on the Internet. A music center can combine many of these items or services under one roof:

1. A virtual CD shop for both new and used CDs, records (some classical music lovers still prefer them to CDs), audio and video cassettes. You can also sell related items and souvenirs such as T-shirts or banners.

2. Music instruction — books, video cassettes, software, online courses.

3. Musicians' supplies: accessories, replacement parts, strings, music sheets, lyrics, simple inexpensive instruments.

4. A referral service for local music schools, studios, instrument dealers, repair services, instrument and sound equipment rentals.

5. Links to similar sites and home pages of musicians/bands.

6. Free information: FAQs, articles written by musicians and experts, visitors' contributions, information about musicians and bands, reviews of new albums.

7. Classifieds: instruments for sale, job opportunities, used records, business opportunities, etcetera.

8. Tickets for local music events.

It is not necessary, of course, to include all the above categories in your site. You may want to concentrate on just one type of music (Rock & Roll, Classical) or service (music instruction).

Start-up investment (other than Internet site costs and connection fees): $20,000+

International potential: Yes.

Special promotional strategies (in addition to those discussed in chapter 5): Link to and from similar sites and sites that attract young adults. Send press releases to music, entertainment, and young adult magazines. Consider holding a quiz on your site (prizes can be CDs, tickets for music events, autographed merchandise).

Qualifications needed: None.

Educating yourself: Magazines, music industry publications and catalogs.

Number of employees needed to start business (apart from yourself): 0

Things to watch out for: You will have to be in tune to the market's trends (especially with rock music). Things change fast in this industry, and unless you keep a watchful eye on "what's hot" you may find yourself stuck with unmovable merchandise.

Additional income: Sound equipment center.

Find a similar business at: http://www.cduniverse.com

120. BROKER FOR ONLINE BUSINESSES

There are several million online businesses currently operating in cyberspace, and their number is expected to grow in at least the proportion of the Internet population growth itself — which means that it will double itself every few years. As with conventional businesses, online businesses open and close, succeed and fail. As with conventional business owners, some online business owners need to sell their businesses.

Selling an online business is easier than selling a conventional business. There is no relocation involved for the new owner, there are no store or office leases to be transferred, and most important of all, it is much easier to track the activity of the business being sold (all sales were transacted via credit cards, direct deposits [e.g., E-cash], or at least checks).

As a business broker for online businesses, you will have a list of businesses who signed a representation contract with you. The fee you charge them is usually 10% of the selling price. Visitors to your site will find a list of all these businesses, which will include such information as: annual gross and net, asking price, reason for selling, number of hits per month, value of inventory (if any), terms. Potential customers will click on the business they are interested in and will be transferred to that business' site. They will also be given e-mail contact addresses or telephone numbers for the owner and for you. However, don't forget to take (and verify) some personal information from such prospects before they are allowed to link to the businesses you represent, so as to make sure that no transaction will be conducted without your knowledge.

Start-up investment (other than Internet site costs and connection fees): $1,000-$5,000

International potential: Yes, with certain limitations. For example, an online shoe store whose warehouse is located in the U.S. will not be able to offer U.S. customers competitive prices if the warehouse was to be moved to Europe and every purchase means overseas delivery.

Special promotional strategies (in addition to those discussed in chapter 5): Send press releases to business, trade and online magazines. Establish links in sites that deal with services for businesses. Send direct land mail to business associations and to CPAs (offer them a referral fee). For paid advertising, consider placing classified ads in "Business Opportunities" sections of major newspapers.

Qualifications needed: Some business background.

Educating yourself: Books and courses. Learn how to read financial reports and how to assess the condition of a business..

Number of employees needed to start business (apart from yourself): 0

Things to watch out for: Don't ask business sellers for an exclusive. This will turn many of them away. You should consult a lawyer during the first months of operations and before you start your business. Don't waste your time on clients who sell their business because it is failing unless the asking price is greatly reduced.

Additional income: Online classified ads.

121. WHO'S WHO DIRECTORY

People like to be mentioned in Who's Who directories. It means recognition, prestige, being associated with important people (if only on paper). Who's Who directories are usually of a local nature, so you will have to divide your site into several geographical areas. Each entry in the directory will include a few lines about the person (the manner of presentation is always positive in such directories), his position, achievements, short biography, and possibly a head shot.

First, you must find prominent residents from every area you intend to cover: business people, entertainers, writers, government officials, politicians, and other affluent or influential people. Once the local VIPs are mentioned in your directory (for free, of course), you can count on many other people who will want to be included in this directory, and who will be willing to pay for it. They may be business people, land owners, educators and people from all walks of life who believe that their achievements and contributions to society are important enough to earn them a mention in the local Who's Who directory. The fee you charge must be small enough to be considered a "one time handling fee" — no more than $20. In addition to the fee, people who want to be mentioned will send you a short biography of themselves, a picture, and a letter asking you to mention their names in the directory. For an additional fee, customers will be able to get a larger space on your site, or special features (for example, an audio file to which they can record a few words).

Another source of income is publishing the complete directory on CD-ROM or in a book form; you can be sure that many of the people mentioned there will be interested in buying it.

Start-up investment (other than Internet site costs and connection fees): $1,000-$20,000

International potential: Yes.

Special promotional strategies (in addition to those discussed in chapter 5): Issue press releases to regional magazines and newspapers. Send direct land mail to local associations and organizations. Key words and descriptions for search engines listings should relate to specific regions (for example, "Connecticut — Who's Who"). When promoting your site, don't forget to mention the names of several local VIPs that are mentioned in your online directory — even if you have to pay them to do this.

Qualifications needed: None.

Educating yourself: Search local directories (business,

government). Subscribe to local magazines and newspapers; read their society columns.

Number of employees needed to start business (apart from yourself): 0

Things to watch out for: Most of the people who will want to appear in your directory cannot be as important or influential as the VIPs you have chosen for forming its basis, but make sure you maintain a certain standard. If visitors to your site are not convinced that the people who appear there are worth mentioning, they would have no motivation to be mentioned there themselves. You may want to check the record of people who want to be included in your site to eliminate practical jokes and false claims.

Additional income: Local society online magazine. Online cemetery.

Find a similar business at: http://www.kaleo.com

GLOSSARY

anonymous FTP site   An FTP site that can be accessed by anyone.

Archie   An Internet feature used for searching files that are located on anonymous FTP sites.

ASCII   American Standard Code for Information Interchange. A system that assigns numeric codes for every letter of the alphabet (and punctuation marks). By using this system, any computer on the Internet can communicate with other computers (at least at the level of simple text messages).

analog line   A simple electric wire that requires digital data to be converted to analog data in order to be transmitted. Telephone lines are analog lines.

auto responder   An e-mail feature that sends an e-mail message to anyone who sends it a blank message (or a message with certain key words). It uses a program called *mailbot*, and its function is not unlike that of a fax-on-demand.

backbone networks   Central networks with high speed computers to which all the other networks of the Internet are connected. Most are maintained by the National Science Foundation.

BBS   Bulletin Board System. A server computer that is connected to a telephone line. It can offer the same services as a Web site, but it is not an integral part of any network.

bps   Bits per second. A unit of transmission speed of electronic data.

browser   A software (e.g., Netscape) that allows Internet users to view World Wide Web sites.

chat programs   Discussion forums that allow users to communicate with each other in real time (unlike e-mail). They can be either text or voice based.

client Any computer that connects to another computer in order to retrieve data from it, or to use its software. A program can also be considered a client. For instance, Mosaic (a type of browser) is a Web client: it utilizes Web features and displays Web information on the user's screen.

cross posting Posting one message to several newsgroups. This practice is sometimes used by commercial enterprises in order to promote their business with unsolicited messages.

cyberspace Although this term has no exact meaning, it is usually applied to the online world or its digital traffic.

dial up account The basic Internet connection that allows individual users to log on to the Internet through a modem.

digital line A high speed line that can transfer digital data without the need to convert it to analog data first. Such lines (e.g., T3, T1) are much more expensive than the regular analog lines, but they allow for much higher transmission speeds.

domain name A combination of letters or numbers that leads to the online address of a computer or a network. The domain name varies according to the Internet feature the addressee is using (Web, gopher), the type of organization (commercial, government) and the addressee's country.

download To copy a file from a remote location (e.g., a server) to the user's computer.

E-cash Electronic cash. A currency that can be exchanged over the Internet. It requires the buyer to purchase the electronic currency from a special bank. The buyer can then use it to purchase goods from Internet vendors who accept E-cash.

e-mail Electronic mail. This feature allows Internet users to send and receive messages.

FAQ   Frequently Asked Questions.

firewall   A security feature that protects networks or computers from unauthorized access by Internet users. Only if you intend to connect directly to the Internet should this concern you (server services will usually take care of this for you).

flame   The e-mail equivalent of hate mail. Such hate messages are usually sent to the victim's e-mail box tens and even hundreds of times. Internet users might do this to businesses that send them unsolicited e-mail.

freeware   Any software that is distributed free of charge for unlimited use (also see: *shareware*).

FTP   File Transfer Protocol. This is a feature that enables the transfer of files (not just ASCII text files) over the Internet.

Gopher   An Internet feature that arranges files under a system of hierarchical directories. It presents users with a clear menu that allows them to search information and even browse through other Gopher sites. Gogherspace is the collective name for all these sites.

hit   A recorded visit (of an Internet user) to a site. If a Web site recorded 200 hits, it means that it was visited 200 times (but not necessarily by 200 different users).

home page   In any Web site, this page functions as the gate. The site's menu is displayed there, plus any general information about the nature of the site.

host   Any computer that allows another computer to retrieve information or access its files.

HTML   HyperText Markup Language. A system of commands that allows a file (document, graphics) to function as a Web page. It allows files other than ASCII to be viewed by Web browsers.

hypertext   When HTML properties are assigned to plain text, it becomes hypertext. Clicking on hypertext will link the user to a different place on the Web page, to a different Web page, or to a different site altogether.

Internet   A collection of about 20,000 networks that connect to several backbone networks.

IP   Internet Protocol. A system of sending and receiving information as a series of independent packets. Naturally, this protocol must be used by any computer that is connected to the Internet.

ISDN   Integrated Service Digital Network. Digital lines that can transfer data at speeds of 64,000 bps+.

LAN   Local Area Network. Any computer network located within the same building or complex. They usually do not have to rely on telecommunication equipment for connection between the LAN's components.

link   A connection between two sites. For example, clicking on a hypertext that reads *"White House"* can take the user to the White House's Web site.

LISTSERVE   An e-mail program that creates and runs mailing lists.

mailbot   See: auto responder.

mailing list   A list of e-mail addresses of people who are interested in receiving messages from a certain source (or from each other). For example, a mailing list set up by a movie fan to let people know of new developments in the movie industry.

Meta file   A file attached to an HTML document that includes data such as title, author, description or key words. Such files can be read by search engines.

modem   A device that converts digital information to analog information (and vice versa) in order to enable such information to be sent over ordinary telephone lines.

newsgroups (a.k.a. USENET newsgroups) A forum that is used by Internet users to post their messages and form discussion groups dedicated to a variety of subjects.

online Any computer that is connected to another computer is "online".

online mall (or virtual mall) A collection of virtual stores under one menu or directory. Sometimes the mall acts as the online businesses' server service, and at other times it only provides links to their site (as well as advertising space).

online world A collective term for all computer networks, whether or not they are a part of the Internet.

packet switching The breaking down of digital information into several packets that travel independently to their destination and reconstruct the complete message once they arrive there. This technology forms the basis of the Internet.

POP Post Office Protocol. This protocol allows Internet users access to their e-mail boxes (which are located on their mail server's computers).

press release A report (on a new site, business, product, book) sent to newspapers and magazines for the purpose of being published by them.

protocol A set of rules by which computers communicate with one another.

search engine An online database that allows Internet users to locate and reach Internet sites.

server See: host.

server service A business that connects directly to the Internet and that rents out space on its computers. By doing so it allows individuals and businesses without a direct connection to the Internet to set up a presence (e.g., Web site) there.

service provider   The connection between the individual and the Internet. The subscriber is connected to the service provider through a modem, and the service provider connects to the Internet through other networks (such as the backbone networks). The subscriber can view Internet sites, but his only online presence is an e-mail box.

shareware   Any software that is purchased on approval. The customer downloads it for a predetermined trial period, and will have to pay the creator if he wants to use it beyond that period.

site   A collection of files (text, graphics) that exists online.

spamming   Posting unsolicited commercial messages to newsgroups, sending such messages to private e-mail boxes, and otherwise engaging in unethical promotional tactics online.

UNIX   The Internet's operating system. Unix is to the Internet what DOS is to PCs.

upload   To copy a file from the user's computer to a remote location (usually a server).

URL   Universal Resource Locator. An addressing system used for finding Web sites.

USENET newsgroups   See: newsgroups.

user (often: Internet user)   A person who logs on to the Internet.

virtual   A common definition of anything that exists only in cyberspace and which has no physical existence: a virtual store, a virtual mall.

virtual Web server   A site that is connected to the Internet through another server in a way that creates the appearance that it is connected directly to the Internet.

WAN   Wide Area Network. A network that is spread over a large distance, even across several different countries. Telecommunication equipment is needed to connect the WANs components.

Web   See: World Wide Web.

Web master   A person in charge of maintaining a Web site; a new job definition in today's corporate America.

World Wide Web (a.k.a. "the Web" or "WWW").   An Internet feature that allows users to view (or download) any file: text, graphics, video, audio, software. It understands various commands that can be given by clicking on an icon or text (see: hypertext).

zine   Online Magazine.

APPENDIX 1

A Partial List of Server Services

All the server services listed here maintain Web sites where you can find information about their services, fees, contracts, etcetera (please note the difference between the (-) and(_) signs, and also between html and htm in the sites' URL addresses).

INTERLINK 2000 WEB SERVICES
P.O.B. 811 Union City TN 38281-0811
Tel 800 972-1250
http://www.interlink-2000.com

INTERNETTER INTERACTIVE
Tel 619 277-6109   Fax 619 277-4654
http://www.internetter.com/service/compare.html

ABACUS WORLD WIDE WEB PUBLISHING
182 Sea Island Pkwy Suite 561 Beaufort SC 29902
Tel 803 838-3955
http://abacus-mall.com/ws&vs.htm

WEBACRES
513 Green St' New Haven IN 46774
Tel 219 749-1137
http://webacres.com/pricelist.html

SEANET CORP.
701 5th Ave. Suite 6801 Seattle WA 98104
Tel 206 343-7828   Fax 206 628-0722
http://www.seanet.com/seanet/commercialweb.html

ACS
7411 Alban Station Court, Suite A104 Springfield VA 22150
Tel 703 866-5500   Fax 703 866-5502
http://www.s6000.com/acs/internet.html

PM GROUP
440 Birch Ave. Eaton CO 80615
Tel 303 454-1548
http://www.java-apps.com/index.html

APPENDIX 2

Useful Links

Traffic measuring services and online advertising agencies:

Doubleclick http://www.doubleclick.net

I/PRO http://quantum.ipro.com

PC-Meter http://www.npd.com

Promotion:

Oregon State University
http://www.orst.edu/aw/stygui/propag.htm

Link Master http://linkmaster.com

American Demographics Inc.   http://www.marketingtools.com

Leading Learning Fountains (awards)
http://www.tricky.com/lfm/awards.htm

Who's Marketing Online   http://www.wmo.com

Virtual Promote   http://www.virtualpromote.com/home.html

Entrepreneurs' resources:

So You Want to Start A Business on the Internet
http://www.actium1.com/home

Babson College (Gopher) http://gopher.babson.edu

Entrepreneurs on the Web http://www.eotw.com//EOTW.html

How to Start a Business
http://www.inreach.com/sbdc/book/index.html

Entrepreneur Weekly http://www.eweekly.com/news

Services for online businesses:

La Sierra University http://www.lasierra.edu/~willgurn/dlist

Searching Gopherspace:

Galaxy
http://galaxy.einet.net/gopher/gopher.html

Checking the availability of domain names:

InterNic http://rs.internic.net/cgi-bin/whois

Issuers of online currency:

DigiCash http://www.digicash.com

Cyber Cash http://www.cybercash.com

What's New services:

WebCrawler http://webcrawler.com/select/nunu.new.html Choose
"Add URL" to include your site.

Consumer World's What's New
http://www.directory.net/dir/whats-new.html (Click on: "How to
submit listings").

What's New Too
http://newtoo.manifest.com/WhatsNewToo/submit.html This
site promises to post your listing within 36 hours.

A Directory of 500 online malls:

http://nsns.com/MouseTracks/HallofMalls.html

Links to over 200 Web directories, Search engines and link services

Go Net Wide   http://www.GoNetWide.com/gopublic.html

INDEX